OVER, UNDER, THROUGH:

Obstacle Training for Horses

Also by Vanessa Bee

The Horse Agility Handbook: A Step-by-Step Introduction to the Sport

Horse Agility: A Step-by-Step Introduction to the Sport (DVD)

3-Minute Horsemanship: 60 Amazingly Achievable Lessons to Improve Your Horse (and Yourself!) When Time Is Short

OVER, UNDER, THROUGH:
Obstacle Training for Horses

50
Effective, Step-by-Step
Exercises for Every Rider

Vanessa Bee

Photographs by Philip Osborne

TRAFALGAR SQUARE
North Pomfret, Vermont

First published in 2015 by
Trafalgar Square Books
North Pomfret, Vermont 05053

Disclaimer of Liability

The author and publisher shall have neither liability nor responsibility to any person or entity with respect to any loss or damage caused or alleged to be caused directly or indirectly by the information contained in this book. While the book is as accurate as the author can make it, there may be errors, omissions, and inaccuracies.

Trafalgar Square Books encourages the use of approved safety helmets in all equestrian sports and activities.

Library of Congress Cataloging-in-Publication Data

Bee, Vanessa.
Over, under, through : obstacle training for horses : 50 effective, step-by-step exercises for every rider / Vanessa Bee.
pages cm
Includes index.
ISBN 978-1-57076-727-2
1. Horses--Training. 2. Horsemanship. I. Title.
SF287.B369 2015
636.1'0835--dc23
2015015922

Photographs by Philip Osborne
Book design by Lauryl Eddlemon
Cover design by RM Didier
Typefaces: Myriad, Minion
Index by Andrea M. Jones (www.jonesliteraryservice.com)

Printed in China

10 9 8 7 6 5 4 3 2 1

This book is dedicated to my horse, Secret, who helped us make this book what it is. Throughout all the photo sessions she never once refused to complete an obstacle, even those she had never experienced before. She has taught me that there's a time to run and there's a time to stand still and think—knowing which one to choose is what we learn through life.

CONTENTS

PART THREE: THROUGH 115

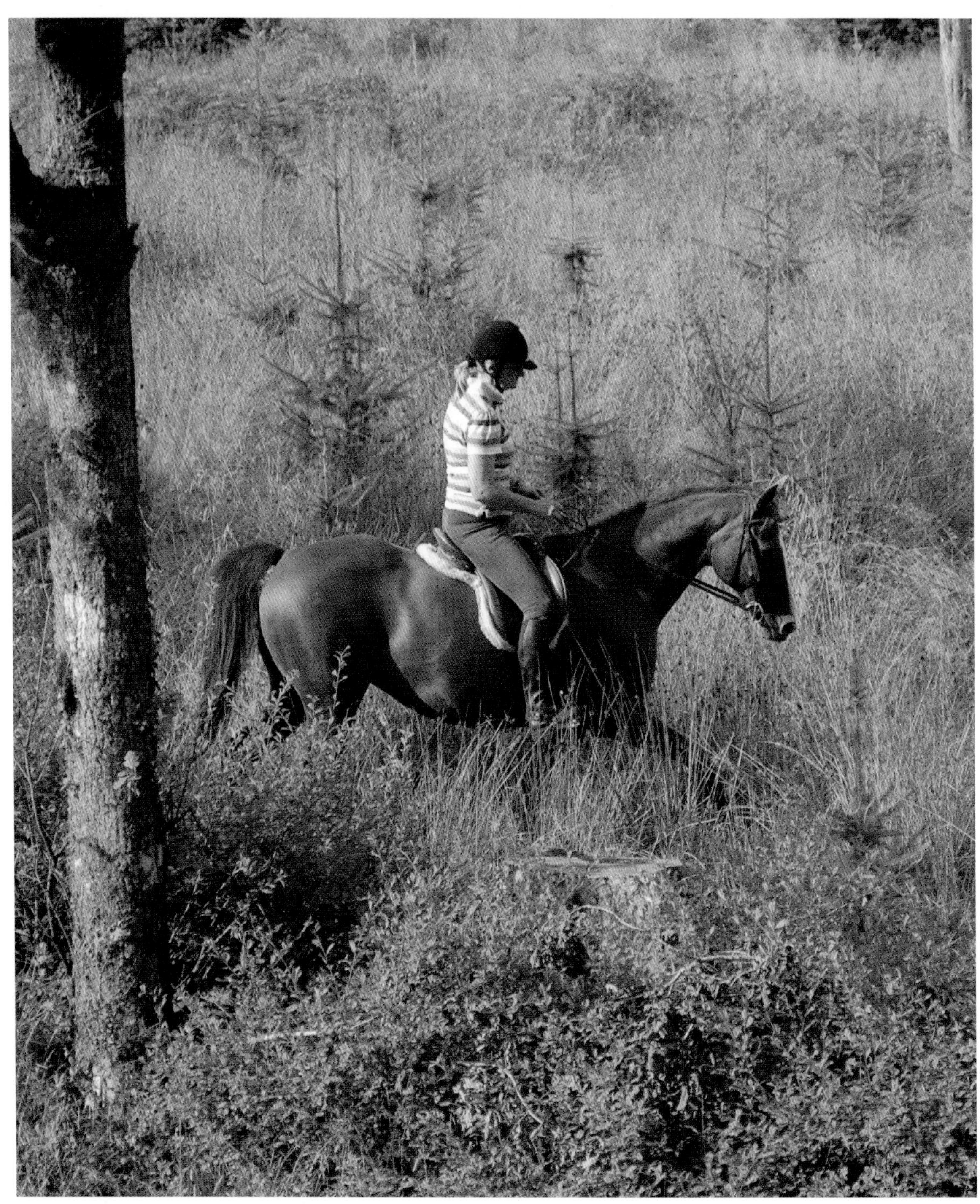

Acknowledgments

An enormous thank you goes to everyone at Trafalgar Square Books for their belief in my ideas and for presenting them in such a clear and accessible way. This book is very much a team effort; they made my dream a reality.

Thank you to my husband Philip for following round after me and my horse Secret as we did the fun stuff, and he took the photos.

Also grateful thanks go to my friends and their horses who kept telling me what fun they were having:

- Emma with her horses Maddy and Flynn for meeting the pigs and herding sheep.
- Carol and Pearas for carrying the Union Jack.
- Amy and Salty for jumping through the hoop.
- Laura and Rowlagh for wading through bottles.
- Jane and Chloe for galloping along the beach.
- Sophie for letting us use her arena when our field became a bog.
- And to Colesmill Stables Holsworthy who were happy to join in the fun at a moment's notice (www.colesmillstables.co.uk).

Introduction

Over thousands of years the human race has done some extraordinary things involving horses. They have ridden on their backs, loaded them into confined spaces and traveled them over land, water and through the air to environments in which no horse would ever choose to stay. The freezing wastes of Antarctica, battlefields with the deafening roar of cannons, city streets filled with smelly, noisy vehicles and people, the list goes on and on. This adaptability in horses shows us that they have an incredible ability to learn about new environments and how to survive within them.

However, despite the fact that we have selectively bred this adaptable animal to be amenable to our way of life, we still meet the horse that reverts to being wild, sometimes at the most inconvenient moments. This varies from horse to horse due to temperament and learned behaviors but there is a factor common to all: they start out working to a three-million-year-old risk assessment, and this trait has never been bred out of them.

In the horse's survival plan when something even slightly resembles a predator he will just run away. But what about rocks, rustling leaves, and flapping birds that our domestic horse spooks at? Surely all these things were there three million years ago and the horse learned that a rock was a rock and wouldn't chase him?

This is where you have to start to think like a horse, see like a horse, feel like a horse. Compare a rock and a crouching lion. They look pretty similar if you take out the color and the shadows and turn them into two dimensional shapes, which is what a horse sees. Rocks, lions, people sitting in chairs, and trash bags all look pretty much like a crouching predator to a horse. He's not going to spend too long making the decision whether to run or stay because his risk assessment says run.

Fortunately, due to the innate adaptability of the horse it is possible to help him rewrite that survival handbook. You can do it by the sink-or-swim method by telling the horse to forget all that risk-assessment nonsense and get used to whatever it is that's scaring him. That is what happened in battle; no one spent hours training the horse to accept gunfire or noisy tanks or deep, water-filled craters. The animals arrived on the battlefield and were immersed in the horror of war. They either adapted or they didn't, and those that didn't were lost.

The other way is to actually help the horse change his survival strategies and bring him into the twenty-first century. Someone needs

to help him rewrite that "Three-Million-Year-Old Risk Assessment" and that's where you come in. Not only is it fascinating to work on together, it increases the trust that you and the horse have in each other and that's the basis for a wonderful relationship.

Why I Have Written This Book

Do you want to take your horse over a course of cross-country jumps having fun and feeling safe?

Do you want ride on a loose rein through forest glades under sweet smelling pines, listening to bird songs?

Do you want to gallop through waves on a sandy beach?

Yes?

Well now you can get started to achieve your dreams.

You may want to start in the arena or paddock but eventually it's great to go out and have some real fun. Riding outside the

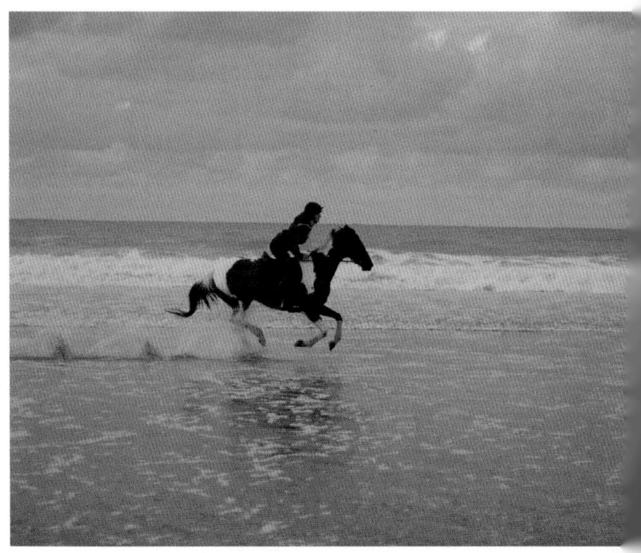

schooling arena is when your horsemanship really begins to shine as you put all that groundwork, obstacle training, and dressage into practice.

Consider opening a gate while on horseback, moving cattle, riding through the sagebrush in rough country, or going to a show where every scary thing known to horses can be found. All those movements you've so carefully perfected in the arena begin to mean something. All the carefully perfected turns-on-the-forehand and hindquarters are there if you need them to pass through gates, work with cattle, or simply make a safe turn as you complete a course of show jumps.

Think of the trust needed between horse and rider to push through thick undergrowth and negotiate the hubbub of a horse show. You could stay in the arena forever perfecting your half-passes, lead changes, and pirouettes but, for me, testing my skills by riding in many different places is what it's all about.

In 2013, England had the wettest, warmest winter for many years and I got a lot of calls from people asking for help with their "dangerous" horses. It transpired that because the ground was waterlogged these horses were not allowed outside in the pasture to let off steam. Most were not being allowed out of their stalls at all except for a short schooling session in the arena once a day, and not always that often.

The horse is an animal that needs to move to remain physically and mentally healthy but here were these large domestic horses standing in stalls 12 feet square for 23 hours a day. No wonder when they were taken out they seemed dangerous, they were just bursting with too much energy. It was only on further investigation that I discovered that even in the summer many of these horses were never ridden outside the arena because, even when they had turnout, they were too spooky to ride. This was in places where there were wonderful rides through open countryside, along bridleways and quiet lanes but the riders were unable to ride these fabulous, athletic horses outside the arena—ever.

What a waste!

It wasn't that many of these riders didn't *want* to ride outside, they just *couldn't* because the horse, and sometimes the rider, couldn't cope. It was time to start helping people and their horses to ride out and so the idea for this book was born.

What Equipment Do You Need?

You should be able to work through this book without buying any specialist equipment for handling or riding your horse, just use your usual gear. However, when working on the ground I always suggest a longer lead rope, at least 10 feet (3m) long so that you and the horse can move without compromising each other's safety. I always recommend that people wear a riding helmet, gloves, and sensible footwear.

For some of the more specific exercises you may need to do a bit of research to source items such as festive decorations, flags, marker cones, footballs (soccer) and umbrellas but these are readily available worldwide. I have tried to keep any extra items inexpensive and easy to make yourself, and these ideas are outlined in the text at the relevant exercise.

What you do not need to have is an arena. I'm almost glad now that I have never had one because it has made me ride out and work with my horse along tracks, roads, and open spaces. If you do not feel ready to do this, and don't have an arena, then create a small fenced-off area in which you feel safe. There is absolutely no reason to start in a great big field. As you begin to feel safer the space can be slowly made larger. This concept will be explored in *Through: Exercise 17*, "Wide Open Spaces," the last one in this book (p. 156).

I really do recommend that you read the book through before you start. The pictures will show you what to look for while the words will explain how to get there. Most of the time you can then just dip in and decide which exercise you'd like to explore, though in some cases I may suggest that you look back at a previous exercise and check that the foundation work is in place.

How to Get Started

It is said that if you ask 20 different horse people the same question you get 20 different answers. So if you asked "How can I ride out safely in open spaces and past spooky objects?" you might hear the following: "Keep your leg on," "Keep your leg off," "Be in charge of the horse," "Let the horse go on a loose rein," "Be the boss," "Sing," "Breathe," "Let the horse look," "Turn the horse away"—in fact, so many different instructions you don't know which one to choose.

Unfortunately, it's usually too late to decide what to do when something scary does happen so let's get you prepared. Whenever I consider a potential "problem" with a horse, I go right back to the very foundations of my horsemanship skills. Here's what I do:

I control my horse's feet!

It's that simple. If I can direct the horse to pick up his feet and place them where, when, and how I want them, I can stay in control in a scary situation. After all, if I can control the feet, the rest of him will follow.

But how can you even start thinking about directing the horse's feet while he is jumping around in fear? Well, the simple answer is you don't start this training until you *can* direct his feet.

Most of us like to think that we are fully in control of our horse but often just manage the world around him so that he doesn't become difficult to handle. We consciously, or unconsciously, keep him away from situations where he might feel afraid or use a gadget to prevent him from physically running away when he does. But every now and again something happens that is totally unexpected and out of our control, and no gadget on earth will keep that horse from running.

What this book is about is educating the horse to see scary things, check in with his handler and rider, and react accordingly. Please note you are not desensitizing the horse (I like my horse sensitive), you are not spook-busting him (I want life in my horse), you are showing him, through a series of exercises, that if he listens to his rider or handler, he will be safe.

The more you practice, the braver you both will become. "Training" your horse to load into a trailer calmly is not something you do on the morning of the horse show. This may seem like common sense but I am constantly amazed at how many people do it. Lack of preparation is the biggest mistake we can make in working around horses because when they get scared, they can get very big!

In this book I have explored a number of common scenarios, but what happens if the very one you want to address isn't here? Well the exciting thing is that the more obstacles or scary things you show the horse, the more trusting and accepting he becomes of things neither you, nor he, have ever seen before.

For example, many years ago I rehabilitated an ex-racehorse called Stanley. We were riding along a quiet country lane when a large farm machine appeared around the corner. It was bright blue and had enormous "crab-like claws" protruding from the front. Stanley and I had certainly never seen such a terrifying beast before. The monster stopped and as we approached I called to the driver and asked him what it did. He told me it was a blackcurrant picker.

Stanley and I inspected the machine before squeezing through between the "claws" and the hedge and went on our way. There is no way we could have prepared for such a specific obstacle but because we had done so much around lots of other odd things, the blackcurrant picker had become just another obstacle: it was generic. Stanley knew that if I didn't get scared then everything was fine, and so did I.

All these exercises start very simply and, easily and gradually, build in challenge. I urge you to only stretch yourself and your horse to the point where you still feel safe. This is not a race, even if you are working through this because your horse is losing competitions through his fearfulness at events. You may need to step away from competing for a while to "fix" the problem. Ultimately, I believe that this will bring you an even bigger prize—the trust of your horse. And there is nothing greater than that!

Why Over, Under, Through?

For many years I have been helping horses come to terms with the world of humans and the sorts of obstacles that bring out the survival instinct, which may be flags, trailers, cattle, or even people. What has become very obvious to me is that the horse is often not afraid of the whole object but just one part of it.

If you examine an obstacle you begin to see that it is made up of one, two, or three elements. It is either *over* something, like a bridge, or *under* something such as a low branch, or *through* something like a gate. Sometimes it can be a combination like a doorway, which is under and through, or a trailer, which is over the floor, under the roof, and through the partitions and sides. If you really observe your horse carefully, you will see that he is not frightened by the whole obstacle, only one bit of it—one element is scarier than the other two.

Let's look at a common example, loading into a trailer or other vehicle.

Have you ever had a horse that would not

step onto the ramp or up onto the floor of the trailer, and after what seems like hours, he rushes up the ramp and stands in the trailer happily munching on his hay? He doesn't like going *over* things.

Have you ever had a horse that walks straight into the trailer then throws his head up hitting the roof and rushes out backward? He's frightened of going *under* the roof.

Have you ever have a horse that walks halfway in, stops, and runs out backward? He doesn't like the feeling of the pressure of the sides of the trailer.

Every horse has a weakness in one of these areas. He may not like walking over a trailer ramp but he'll also have trouble crossing bridges, tarpaulins, and walking over other changes in surface. Once you know which element your horse doesn't like, you can present him with many different types and it will eventually become generic. In other words, you will help him rewrite his Three-Million-Year-Old-Risk Assessment that says everything that you have to walk over is dangerous. By working on the exercises in this book you not only will be able to identify that weakness, you and your horse can work together on bringing him into this century.

Sometimes it was difficult to know which section to place the obstacle as it had elements of all or some of *over, under,* or *through* so I chose the one I felt was more obvious than the others.

In some of the photographs you can see I have put colored markers on my horse's legs. This means you can read through the text and refer to the photo more quickly without having to work out if I'm referring to the horse's right, the reader's right, the handler's right, or remember which is the near or off side. The horse's right foreleg and left hind leg are marked with pink bandages; the left foreleg and right hind leg have blue bandages.

In horseman's terms, the pink pair of legs is called the *right diagonal* and the blue pair of legs is called the *left diagonal.*

Six Blueprint Exercises

As you work through all the exercises you will need to ensure that you have some foundation skills in place. I have isolated just six that I encourage you to work through before you start, or refer back to, when they are mentioned within an exercise as an aid to success. These *Blueprint Exercises* will help you move your horse forward, backward, and yield the hind and front end smoothly and easily, with the final *Blueprint Exercise* actually showing you how to stop your horse in an emergency.

The six Blueprint Exercises are:

1 Leading Forward
2 Stop and Back Up
3 Advance and Retreat
4 Move the Hind End Around
5 Move the Front End Around
6 The One-Rein Stop/Emergency Stop

Leading Forward (p. 8)

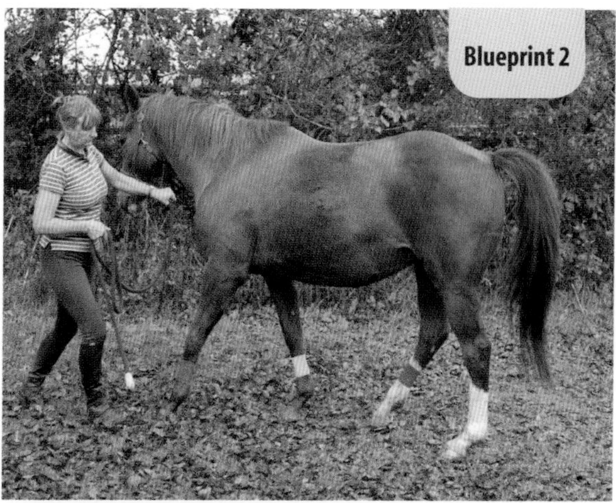

Stop and Back Up (p. 9)

Advance and Retreat (p. 11)

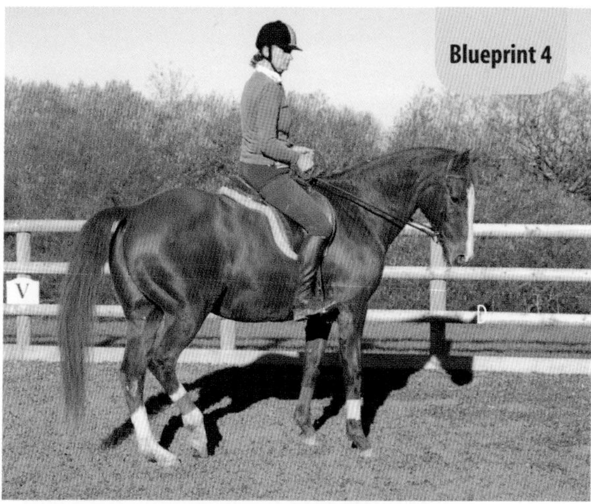

Move the Hind End Around (p. 14)

Move the Front End Around (p. 17)

The Emergency Stop Rein (p. 20)

A

B

BLUEPRINT 1: Leading Forward

Leading a horse is much more than attaching him to the end of a rope and expecting him to know that he is to stay with the handler. The horse has to be shown how to react to the rope and feel how it communicates with him. It's really important not to drag on a horse because this actually causes him to go more slowly as he pulls back. Dragging and pulling on some horses can cause them to feel trapped and claustrophobic, thereby inducing panic.

Allow the horse to travel along, following the feel of the rope. It is so much easier than getting into a pulling match that will ultimately end with the horse winning. (I have not addressed riding the horse forward as most people are quite able to achieve this.)

C

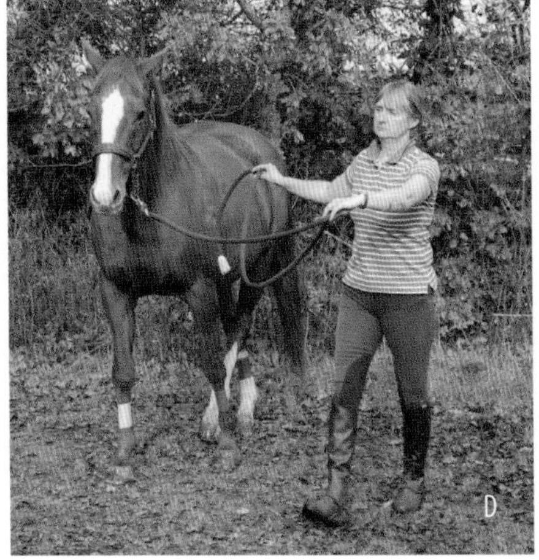
D

A Stand at the girth area; this is where you will be when you ride. Decide what you are going to use to mean "Walk" and stick to it, as the horse follows the instruction and you both move freely forward together.

B If the horse does not walk, change hands with

the rope and really open up the leading hand so that he can feel as if the front door is open.

C Give him time to think but if he still isn't moving, swing the end of the rope towards the girth area about where your foot would be if you were riding.

D If he still does not move, bump the area behind the elbow about where your foot would be until he makes the slightest move forward, then stop.

E Sometimes you might need to change your leading position to give the horse confidence to go over, under, or through an obstacle. Don't pull on him; invite him forward.

F As soon as he feels confident, release the rope. Aim to return to the side of your horse as soon as you both feel ready. If you always lead in front of your horse he may not have the confidence to travel forward when you are on his back.

BLUEPRINT 2: Stop and Back Up

If you can back up your horse, you will find stopping much easier. When a horse backs up correctly he engages his hind end, rocking his weight back as he steps. When a horse stops he makes exactly the same maneuver, which is why they are connected here. If you get a good backup, you will get a much better stop.

You are relating the ground work to your ridden work so don't be tempted to do this by touching the horse's chest or wiggling the rope. You need the horse to release at the poll and raise his withers so that his hocks are engaged. (I have not looked at this as a ridden exercise as in my experience most people can achieve this.)

A Hold the lead rope under the chin with your thumb down. This means your elbow can keep the horse's head straight and you have much more control over the movement. Rock your hand from side to side. Do not push back towards the chest of the horse: he will either over bend or push back towards you and both movements lock up the poll. Each time the horse takes a step, stop rocking your hand then ask again for another step.

B The horse moves backward in diagonal pairs. This is called the right diagonal: the pink front and pink hind are moving together.

C This is the left diagonal: the blue front and blue hind move together. If the pairs do not move together it is not a backup, just backward.

D Once your horse can back up you can work on the stop. Walk with the horse, stop walking and if he does not stop, raise the rope until he feels it bump under his chin.

E If the horse still does not stop, keep bumping the rope upward until he does. Do not pull because if the horse pulls back you are into a pulling match that he will always win. As soon as he stops, you must stop bumping.

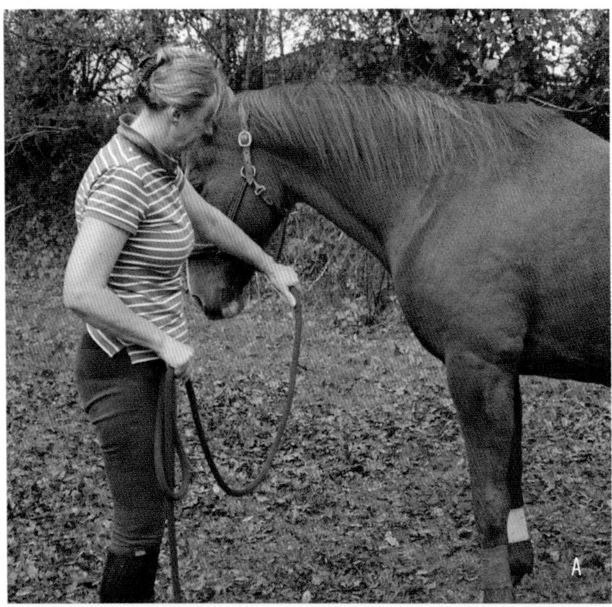
A

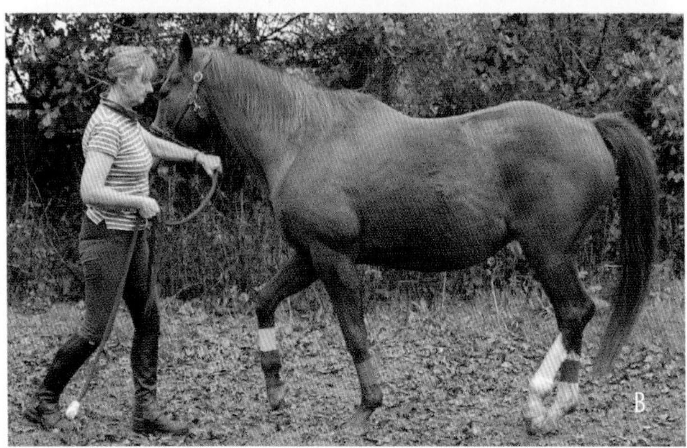
B

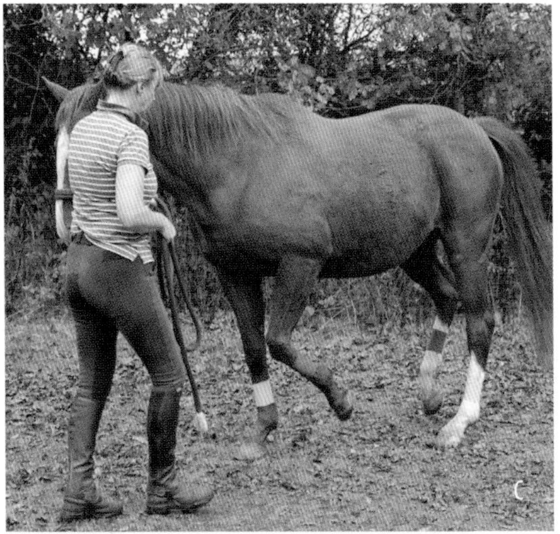
C

D

BLUEPRINT 3:
Advance and Retreat

Advance and Retreat is a method used to help horses slowly, and safely, come to terms with new objects. The idea is that the handler offers a new object for the horse to inspect without scaring the horse to the point where he wants to run away. The handler stays and offers the new object until the horse makes a positive change such as looking at the object, sniffing it, or just relaxing. This relaxation can be shown as the horse starting to blink, right through to the horse relaxing his neck and dropping his head. Every horse is different.

A Use a small flag to get your horse used to flapping fabric. Do not do too much or you may not be able to keep the horse with you.

B When the horse moves away, do not remove the flag. Leave it there until he shows a change, which means he is beginning to accept it.

C Here the horse has made a positive change and relaxed.

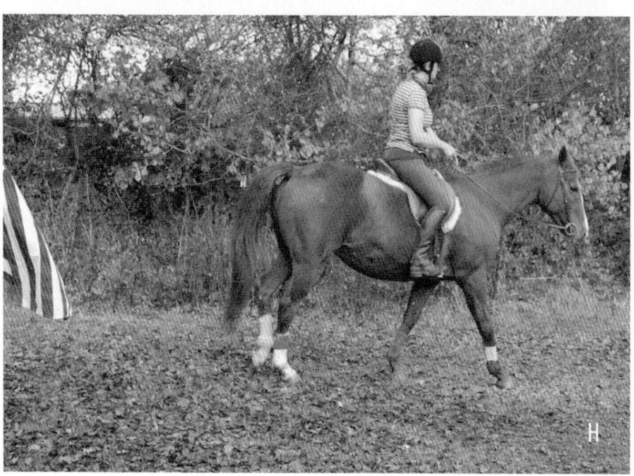

D So I give him peace to let him know that all is well.

E Now the horse is moved towards a flag instead of the flag towards the horse. With much bigger objects, for example a trailer, it is easier to move the horse than the object.

F When he accepted the flag at this distance I move him away to take the pressure off.

G Now I repeat the process from the saddle. Start with the stationary flag and ride towards then away from it, feeling when the horse makes a positive change. Continue to Advance and Retreat towards the flag.

H Ride away when he is calm.

I You could ride in a spiral away and towards the flag, advancing and retreating as your horse makes a positive change.

J Now I pick up the smaller flag and use Advance and Retreat to help my horse accept it.

K I take it away as he shows acceptance.

L If your horse finds a particular object frightening, make it a place of comfort and peace.

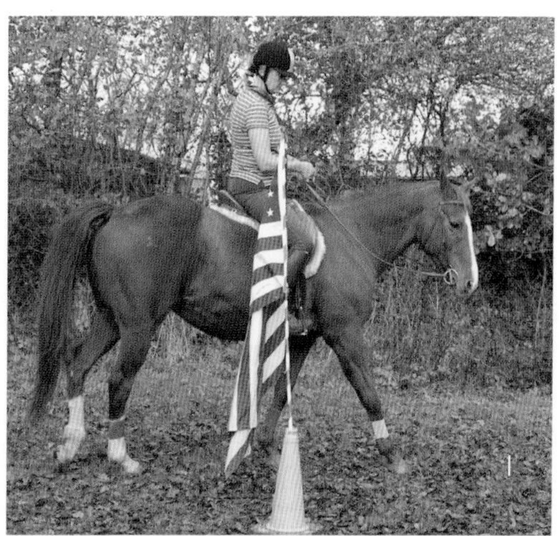
I

J

K

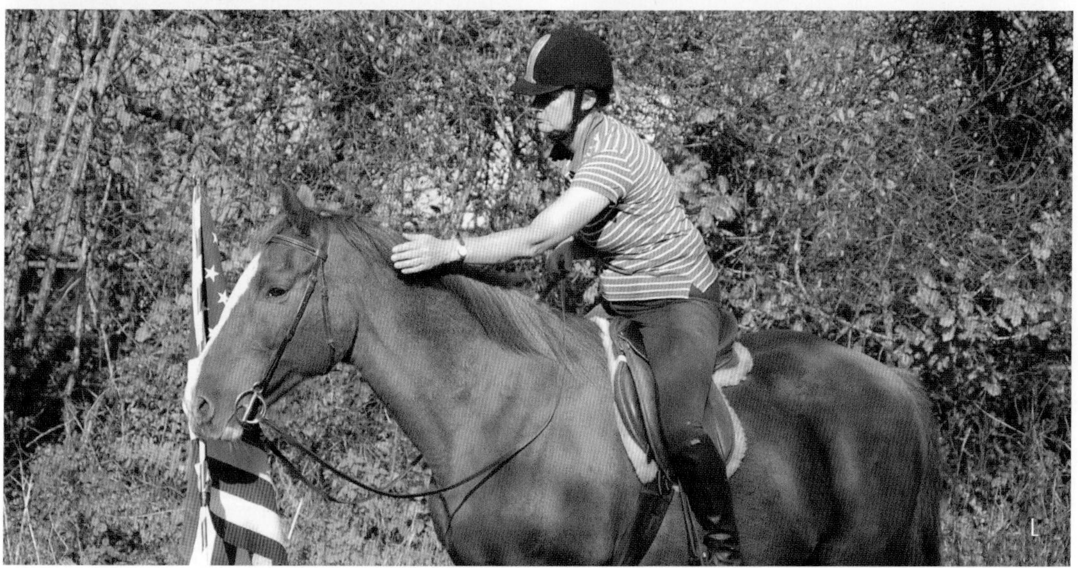
L

BLUEPRINT 4: Move the Hind End Around

The horse's brakes are in the hindquarters so if you can choose when to move them around, you are in much more control of the horse. As with all these *Blueprints*, the work you do on the ground is related to how you ask the same thing when in the saddle.

You are really thinking about moving the barrel of the horse, the rib cage, over and out of the way of the hind leg you want to move. This is what your heel does when you ride: it moves the rib cage to create a space for the hind leg to step into. When you put your heel on the side of the horse, you need to make sure your other heel is out of the way otherwise the ribs cannot move over without pushing into your leg.

A Stand at the side of your horse and ask him to bring his nose around to you. This is called *"lateral flexion."* Do not pull. Put a little tension on the rope until he releases at the poll then release back. You may only get a tiny movement to start with; just ask again until the nose is right around.

B Run your hand down the horse's side until it is where your heel would be if you were riding.

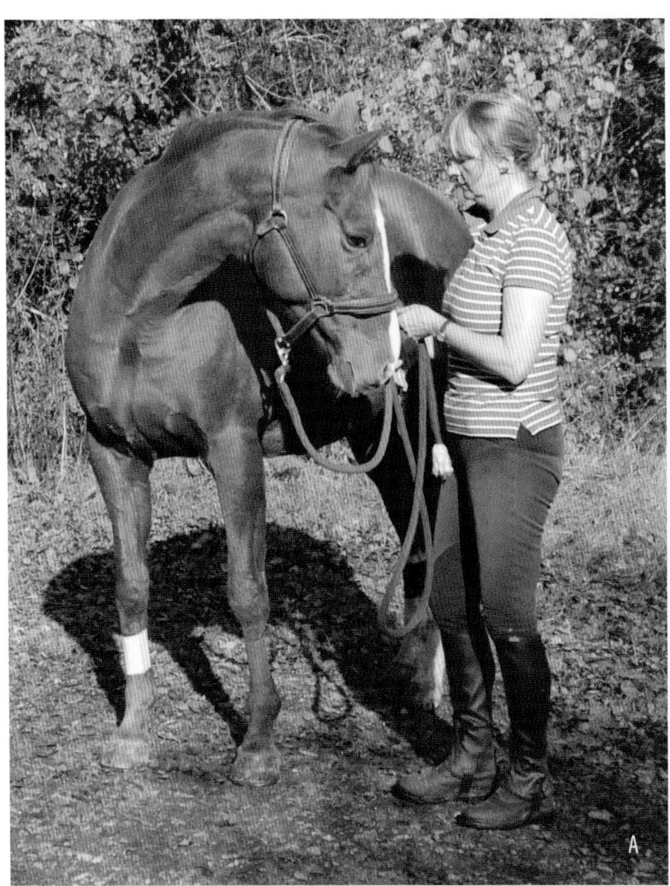
A

B

C

C Now activate the hand and think of the ribs of the horse rolling away from you, which creates a space for the pink hind foot to step underneath. Notice my high-rein hand helping him shape his body up to do this.

D The pink hind foot is now on the ground and the blue hind leg has stepped out; the horse is rearranging his front feet to be able to take the next step.

E The blue hind foot is now placed on the ground and the pink hind foot is about to step under.

F Here the pink hind foot steps over, but be aware that the horse is beginning to lose the flexion in the neck, which is reflected in the pink hind foot not stepping right under the belly.

G Now I am going to ride the same maneuver in the opposite direction. Get the flexion first: here the horse is arranging her feet to get

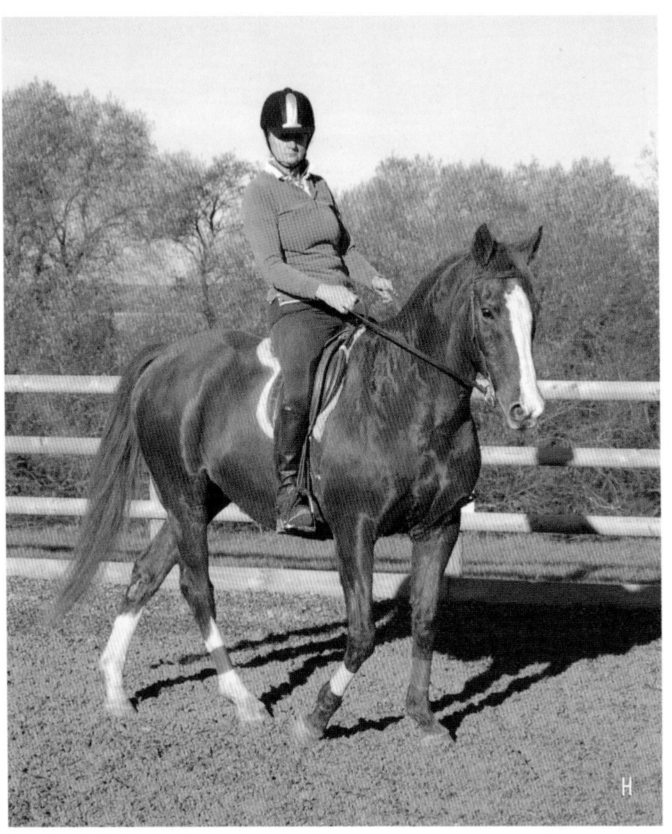

H

started. I want the blue hind foot to step underneath so I put my right leg on her side to move the rib over to make room for it.

H The blue hind foot steps underneath and a little flexion is lost here. I do not keep my leg on throughout this sequence; I release it whenever the horse is committed to the step under with the blue hind.

I The pink hind has stepped down; the next foot to move is the blue hind.

J The blue hind steps underneath. You can see my left leg is off the horse's side to give the barrel a space to move into because my right leg is on her other side moving the rib over to create space for the blue hind to step under.

K The pink hind leg steps under.

I

J

K

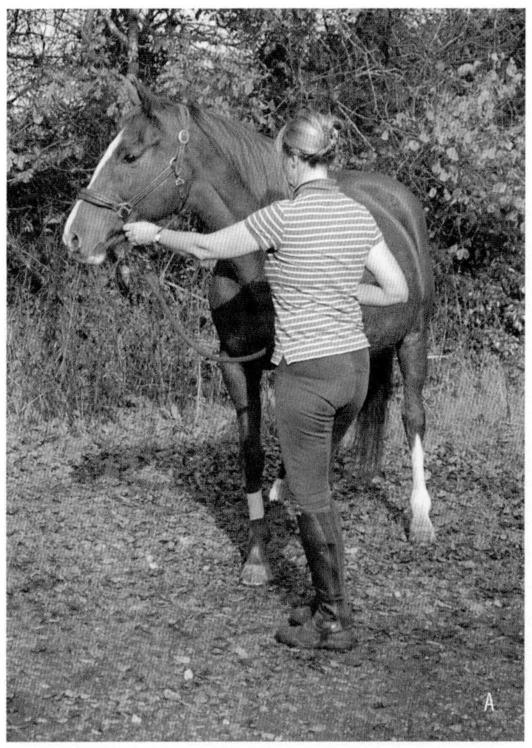

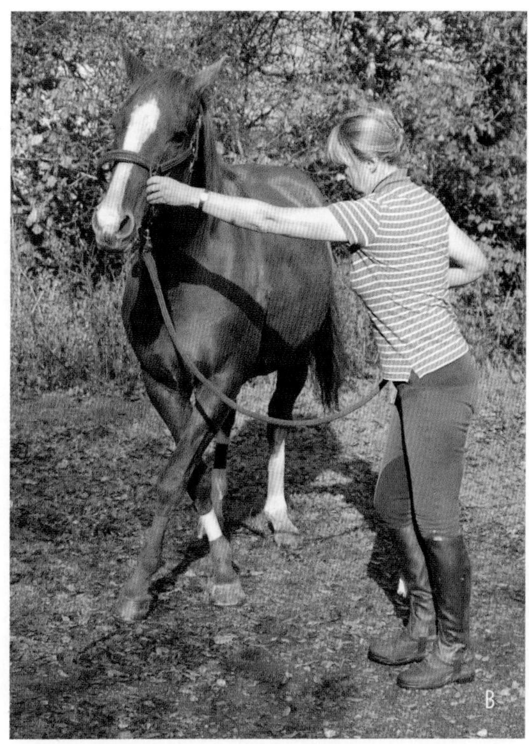

BLUEPRINT 5:
Move the Front End Around

To be able to move a horse's front end easily you need to make sure his weight is off the front. In the beginning it is sometimes easier to ask the horse to take a couple of steps backward before you ask the front end to move because this takes the weight over the hocks and off the front end. Eventually you will be able to just ask the horse to rock back without moving his feet but you may not start here.

A Hold the halter next to the lower jaw and ask the horse to flex away; it should be loose and easy like a newly oiled hinge.

B Here the horse is not flexed away but braced against my hand; you cannot do anything until you have flexion.

C Once you achieve soft flexion you are ready to move the horse's feet. Slightly increase the pressure against the lower jaw by raising your

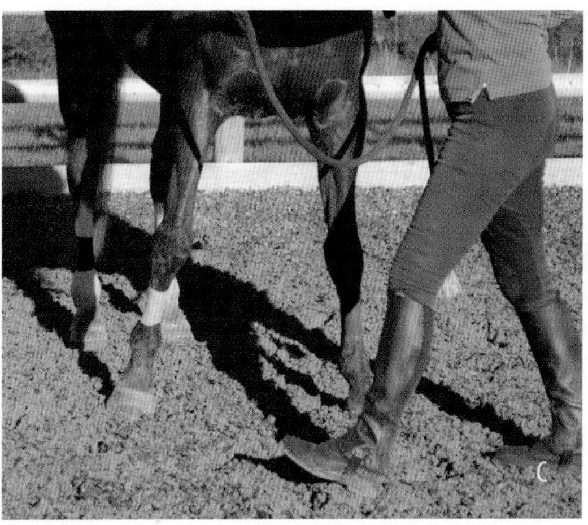

D

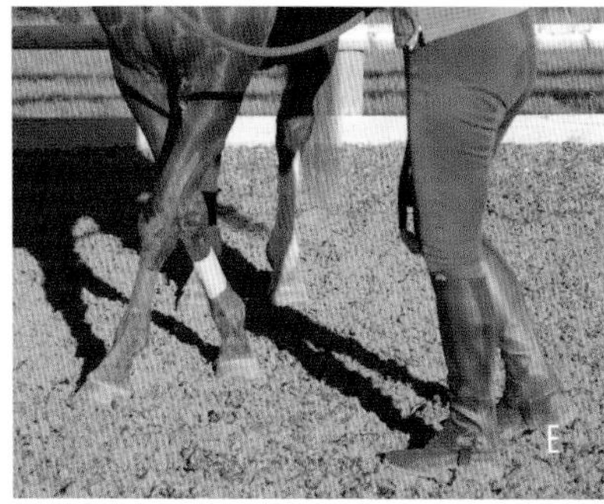

E

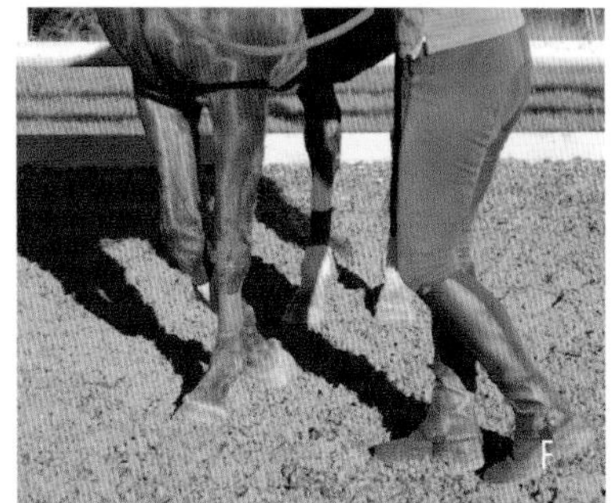

F

G

H

I

J

energy. You are actually asking the blue foreleg to step in front of the pink foreleg. (This photo was taken from a sequence of steps and the pink front foot has just been set down.)

D Here the horse has put his weight on the pink foreleg to free up the blue foreleg to be able to move.

E The horse steps across.

F The horse now has the weight on the blue front foot and the sequence starts again.

G Now we will work from the saddle. Here the horse is taking a step back to set up the feet to step the blue foreleg out to the side. The pink diagonal is stepping back here to take the weight off the blue front foot so that it can step out.

H The pink diagonal is set down and blue foreleg is free to step out. The horse is now able to make the turn because the pink hind foot is taking the weight of the horse.

I The blue front foot steps over; I have lifted my rein on that side to help it move. If you relate this to the ground work you'll remember that after you had the flexion you put pressure on the lower jaw to cause the front foot on the other side to move. This is what the bit is doing here.

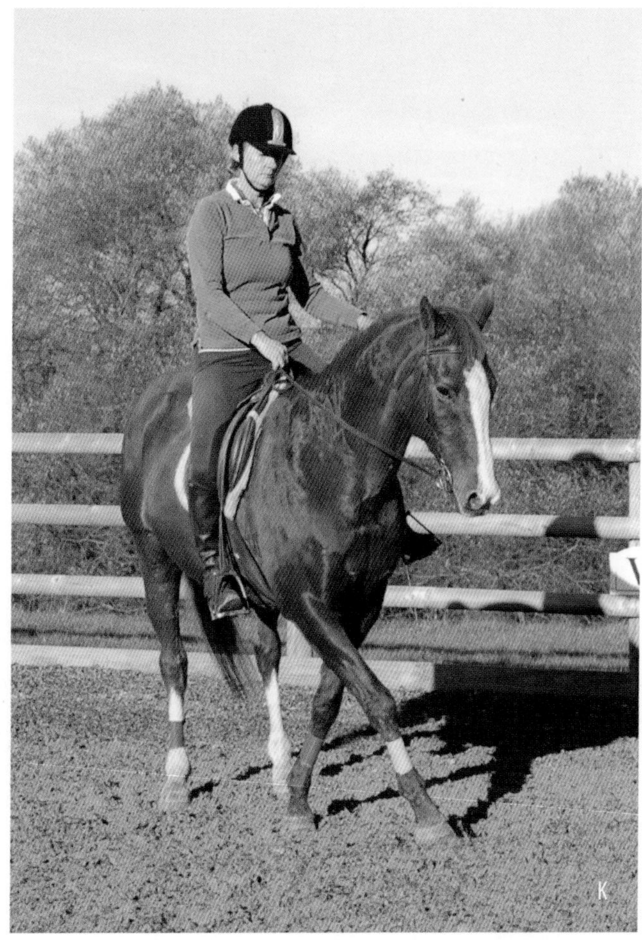

J For the next step, the horse puts the weight onto the blue foreleg and prepares to pick up the pink foreleg. Notice my right foot and right rein are against the horse, my left leg and left rein are away from the horse thus creating a space for him to move into.

K The pink foreleg steps across.

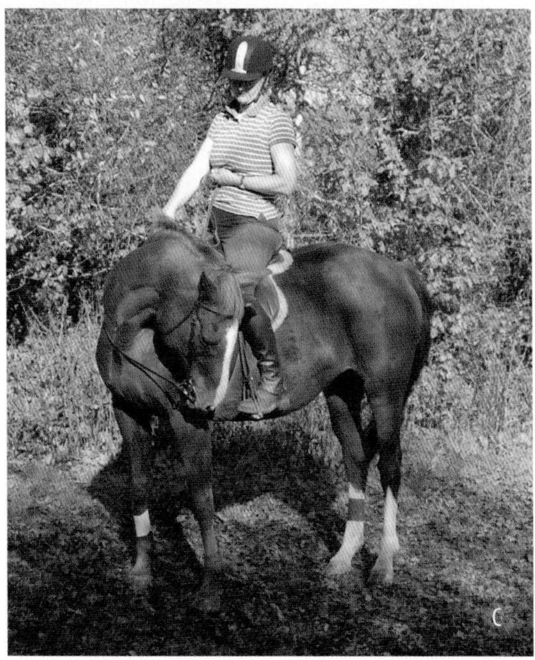

BLUEPRINT 6: The One-Rein Stop/Emergency Stop

This stop is one of the most important things I was ever taught because it gave me access to the brakes on the horse. I get it well established on the ground with any youngster before I take that first ride because if anything scares him I know I can stop him: safely and quietly. For a horse that's already under saddle, it is good to know that in an emergency you can get stopped quickly, but you do need to practice it first. This isn't something you learn from a book and only implement in an emergency. Get so good at this that it becomes second nature when you haven't got time to think in an emergency.

A Bring the hand out and ask for a flex: the rein being away from the neck creates a space for the horse to bend into.

B Sometimes you just have to wait after you have asked. The horse is braced here, and I just hold steady and wait for the release.

C There's the release. After I released back I have moved my hand to my belly button because now I'm going to ask the horse to move.

D With my hand at my belly button and my left leg on the rib I am asking the pink hind leg to step underneath. This will bend the whole horse.

E Keep asking for the pink hind leg to step underneath until the whole movement feels soft as the horse releases.

F Here's a real life scenario. I am out on the trail and my horse starts heading for the gate without my permission. I do not pull on two reins, I reach out with the left hand and begin the one-rein stop.

G I ask for the flexion, though you may not have time to be polite about this as in your practice sessions. In fact, sometimes you might haul the nose round with all the strength you have to get that horse stopped.

D

E

F

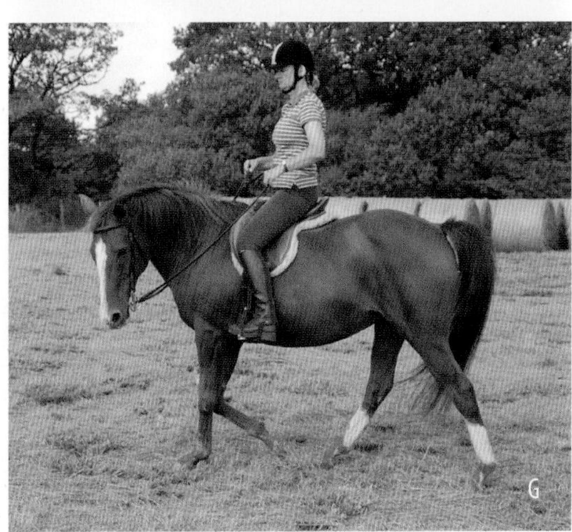
G

H The horse begins to bend but you can see by her twisted head that she has not released.

I The horse begins to soften, the hind leg is stepping under and she begins to let go of the brace at the poll.

J I keep asking until I feel the horse release completely.

K I ride through the softness to a stop. By releasing my rein and taking my leg away, I give the horse peace.

L Then we ride on as if nothing happened.

H

I

J

K

L

The Magic Figure Eight

You need to be able to move the feet where and how you want them, anytime and anywhere. Let's start with a simple exercise moving the horse in a figure-eight pattern. As you understand how your horse moves his own feet, you can begin to influence how to move them.

Don't worry if to start things get pretty chaotic. When I first began this exercise with my horse I thought that just going on the other side and leading her around would be easy, but she really did not want me on her right side. We had a few times when she barged me and pulled away. This really amazed me because I thought I always did things pretty evenly on both sides but she showed me how one-sided we were. It took three or four sessions for her to realize it was safe for me to sometimes appear on her right side.

Sometimes she crowded me (A).

At other times she pulled away (B).

Place two markers about 10 to 13 feet (3 to 4m) apart. This distance depends on the size of your horse. You will be walking beside him to start with so don't make them too far apart.

This exercise is like whisking lumps out of custard or pancake batter. To start, the mixture feels uneven but as you move the lumpy liquid about, it becomes smooth. You will find as you move the horse around the figure-eight the leading becomes smoother and easier.

A You must start this exercise on the ground with just halter and lead rope.

B Starting on the near side of the horse, next to the blue foreleg, walk a figure eight around the two markers, keeping yourself between the horse's cheek and his withers using a loose lead rope.

C Continue to walk the pattern until you have completed a figure eight while maintaining the leading position without the rope going tight as it has in this picture.

D The horse should never crowd you as he is doing here. The figure should feel smooth and even.

A

C

B

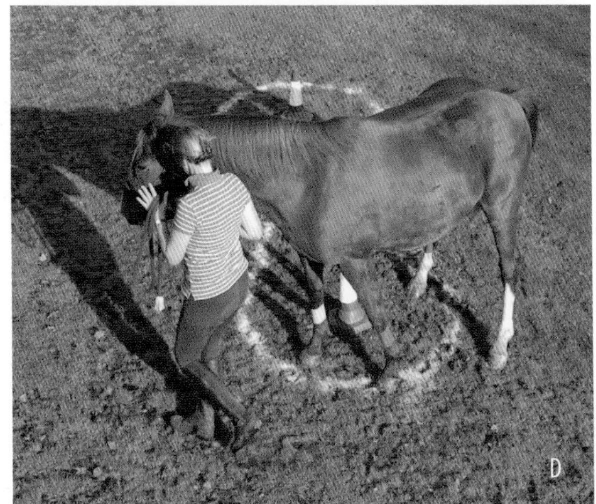
D

E When you feel you have achieved everything in Steps A to D, stop and give your horse a rest for a minute or two before going onto Step F.

F Staying on same side, next to the blue foreleg, walk the figure eight in the opposite direction, obeying all the rules as before until you have walked a smooth figure eight.

G Change sides of the horse. You are now on the off side next to the horse's pink foreleg. Stay between his cheek and withers, retaining a loose lead rope as before.

H Continue to walk the pattern until the figure eight is smooth and even, with the rope never going tight.

E

F

G

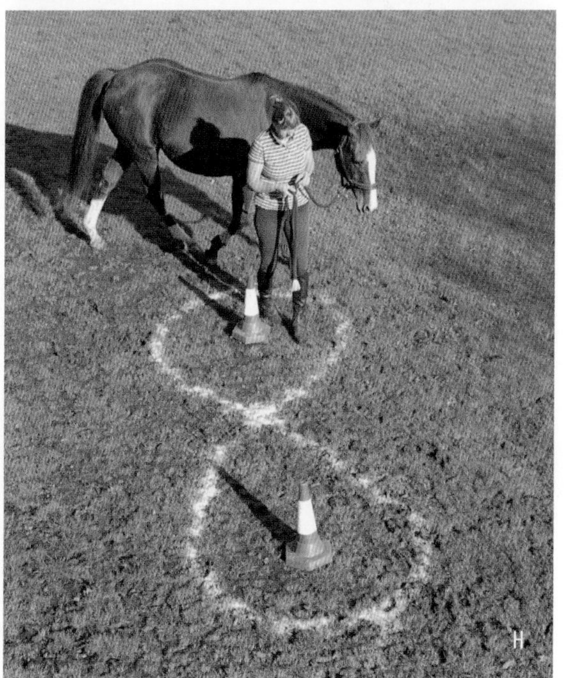
H

I As before, the horse should never crowd you and you should maintain the leading position throughout a complete figure eight. When it feels smooth and even, stop and rest before continuing. In this picture I have adjusted my position because my horse has dropped back on the turn.

J Staying on the same side of the horse, next to the pink foreleg, remain between the cheek and the withers with a loose lead rope and walk the figure eight in the opposite direction.

K Continue to walk the pattern until the figure eight is smooth and even, the rope never goes tight (as it is in the picture), and the horse never crowds you. You must maintain the leading position throughout a complete figure eight before stopping.

I

J

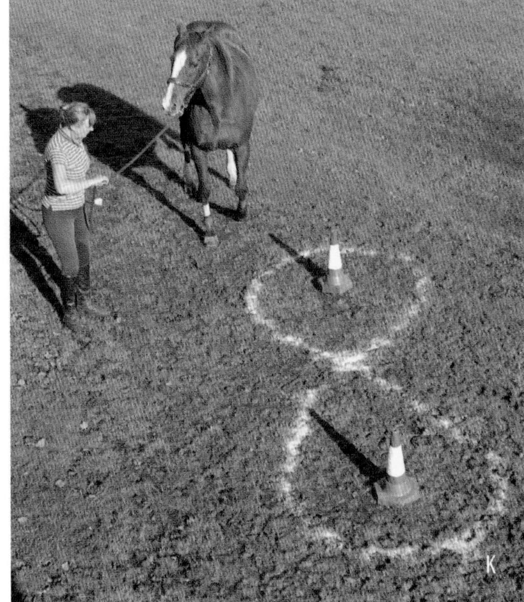
K

The Stuck Foot

As you are completing this exercise become interested in the places where the horse puts the figure eight out of shape. Is it always in the same place? Is it towards the gate or away from a scary object? Or is it when a particular foot is moving?

This is the interesting part to this exercise: Most of the time you will find when a particular foot is the next one to move, the figure-eight becomes lumpy and uneven. By changing sides and directions while completing the same pattern, you can begin to feel which foot doesn't seem to move as freely as all the others regardless of which direction you are going or which side you are on. I call this the "Stuck Foot."

It's like a four-wheeled vehicle with one of the wheels unable to move because the brake on that wheel has jammed on. When that happens the whole vehicle cannot move even though the other three wheels are loose and free. Just imagine if that wheel suddenly stopped moving while the vehicle was actually driving forward. Well, all sorts of interesting maneuvers could happen.

Think about your horse's feet moving along like four nicely oiled wheels. What happens when one foot stops moving? It's likely the three other feet will keep on moving. The least dramatic effect is that the horse will just swivel around the stuck foot drilling it into the ground, but at the other end of the scale a stuck *front* foot can cause a buck, and a stuck hind foot can result in the horse rearing.

It was working with wild horses that taught me this. When I was showing them how to lead they would sometimes get "stuck" and seemed unable to move. I began to observe that in each individual animal it was always one particular foot that seemed to stop moving. So, instead of just getting stronger on the horse to get him to move, I had to work out how to free that stuck foot without pushing or pulling on him. So I learned how to move the hind and front feet separately on the ground as I demonstrated in *Blueprints 4 and 5* (pp. 14-19).

As you lead your horse in the figure-eight observe which foot is his "Stuck Foot." If you find this difficult to do while leading you can video the pattern to watch later, or ask a friend to call out when she sees which foot isn't moving as well as the others.

So once you know which foot isn't moving well how do you fix it?

When it is a front foot, it is easiest to start on the opposite side from the stuck foot. So if it is the pink front foot that is stuck, I position myself next to the blue foreleg. As I am leading my horse in the figure-eight I watch when that "sticky" pink foot is the next to step and influence the way in which it moves as it is about to leave the ground. Once it is placed on the ground, the horse cannot move it because his weight is on it.

If the horse has stopped completely, you need to refer to *Blueprint 1* to encourage the horse to step forward, then get in time with his feet again (p. 8). If the horse steps in towards you then you need to influence the direction of movement of the foot away from you so that the horse does not barge into your space. Refer to *Blueprint 5* to see how to do this (p. 17).

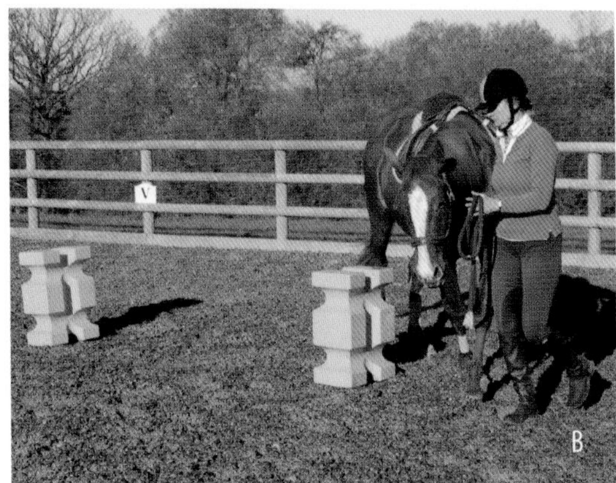

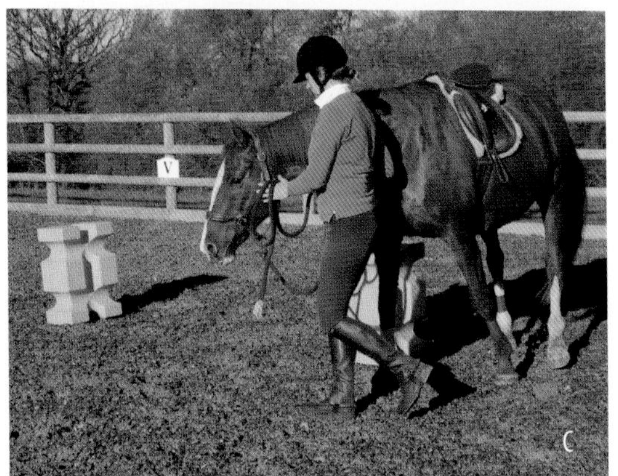

You can see an example of this in this sequence of photos.

A Here I am having to guide the horse away from me. I could feel her slowing down as she prepared to push into me because she was not prepared to step over and therefore remained traveling straight.

B If I do not tip her nose away from me here, she will barge me with her shoulder.

C I am timing that push with the moment her pink foot comes off the ground so that she steps out and away from me and I have influenced the movement of the foot. How you move the front end of the horse over like this is outlined in Blueprint 5 (p. 17).

When it is a back foot the horse usually slows right down or stops moving at all. I would refer to Blueprint 1 (p. 8) here to cause my horse to move up and lead freely beside me. That is, I would drive him forward from behind his elbow as this activates the hind feet.

I could write a book ten times larger than this one on the subject, but if you can just start to watch and feel how your horse's feet move and how you can influence that movement, it will be a good start.

Now that you have some idea which foot is not as free as the others, you can begin to ride the figure eight and to influence that movement while in the saddle.

Riding The Magic Figure Eight

Many of you have ridden figure eights and know how useful the exercise is to warm up a horse before moving onto more intricate exercises. Now I've begun to understand why this ridden pattern actually works. It frees up the feet.

The setup is exactly the same as when you walked the figure eight on the ground but you may want to move the markers to a suitable distance for your horse's length of stride at a ridden walk.

Now ride the figure-eight pattern, trying to retain a loose rein and creating a smooth even pattern.

A First in one direction.

B Then in the opposite direction.

Be interested in the places where the horse creates an uneven pattern. Is it the same as when you were leading him?

C Now that you are beginning to see where the horse's feet get stuck, you can start to ride him round the corners rather than just let him fall in around them.

A

B

C

D As on the ground, I am having to really think about getting in time with the movement of that pink foot so I can “‘pick it up” and move it over as we go around the marker. *Blueprint 5* will help me here (p. 17).

E On the next turn around, I am ready for it and influence the way in which the foot moves as it comes off the ground.

When it is a back foot that is sticky, you will feel the horse push against your leg as he has not rolled his ribs away for the stuck foot to step underneath his belly to make the turn. *Blueprint 4* will help you here (p. 14).

Timing is everything and you will get it wrong quite a bit, so just keep practicing and playing around with it as shown in *Blueprints 4* and *5*. You’ll know when you’ve got it right because the horse will move smoothly and easily.

As I have already said, there are thousands of words and pictures that could be put together here but really the very best way is to become aware of what is happening with the feet: feel it and fix it. No amount of watching or reading can get you there. Just like any skill, it takes practice and dedication to get good at being in charge of your horse’s feet.

Once you know what your horse feels like when he is moving freely and how he feels when his feet are getting sticky, you will begin to feel how this becomes magnified when the horse is afraid.

If it’s a front foot, he is more likely to buck as the front foot stays where it is and all the other feet keep moving. Think of the car with a stuck front wheel and you’ll begin to understand what is happening (see p. 27).

If it’s a back foot, he is more likely to rear. He drops his head and pushes off with one of his front feet before he goes up. I call this the secondary stuck foot, when he pivots on the diagonally opposite hind foot. This is why horses that suddenly spook will often turn in the same direction; they are pivoting over a stuck hind foot.

When your horse stops or threatens to buck or rear you could randomly try freeing up each foot, but it's so much easier when you know which foot it is likely to be so that you can immediately start work on that one before the action really gets out of control.

The really useful thing about this pattern is that it can help calm down a worried horse when practiced at home until it is solid. Many of my students immediately begin the *Magic Figure Eight* exercise on the ground as soon as they arrive at an event and only move on to riding it as the horse settles. The results have been like magic bringing a horse's attention comfortably back to his handler because he has a familiar "job" to do.

Riding The Magic Figure Eight Outside The Arena

If you feel ready to ride outside the arena, I really encourage you to find some natural obstacles to ride your figure eight around. Here we have a beautiful beech wood with good footing and lots of trees at various distances apart. I often ride out there and spend time weaving through the trees. I imagine my reins are hooked onto my horse's front feet and that my feet are connected to my horse's hind feet as I feel her barrel swing in time with their movement. I find it a wonderfully peaceful thing to do. I forget the outside world and just get in touch with my horse's feet.

A The trees grow naturally with many different spaces to weave through.

B I am trying to get in time with the front foot nearest the camera to pick it up and step it towards the camera.

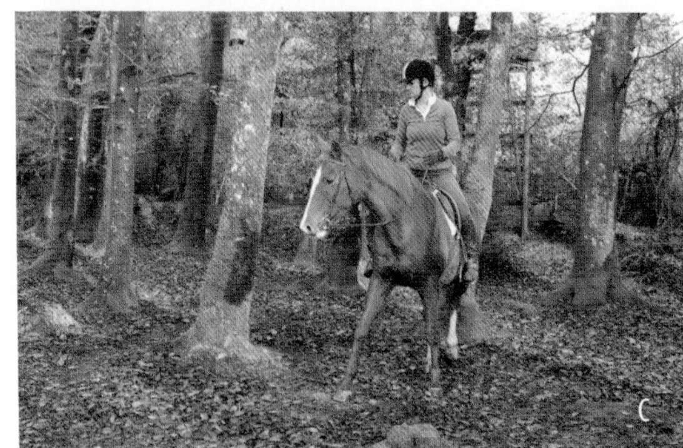

C I have moved my horse's foot up and out to the side.

D My dog, Kestrel, often joins me on rides in the forest.

Thinking Like a Horse

Horses are not frightened of everything, they are frightened by change. But when you think about it, horses can get used to anything.

We tried an experiment with my horse placing various objects that are very familiar to her out on the trail to see how she would react to them. Without exception she looked at them with great suspicion before approaching cautiously.

She isn't being stupid when she does this—she's being a horse.

The other interesting thing is if I rode her in the opposite direction past the object she would behave again as if she'd never seen it

before. This has everything to do with how the horse's brain and eyesight are wired. When a horse sees something out of one eye, it registers on one side of his brain; if you turn him round and look at the same object out of the other eye, his brain doesn't have any record of this experience so he behaves as if he hasn't seen it before.

Let's think about a human equivalent of this situation. I have a suitcase at home that I use for traveling. It's an ordinary battered piece of luggage that has traveled many thousands of miles with me. There are lots of suitcases like this all over the world that carry clothing and supplies as people travel. There's nothing scary about a suitcase, is there?

Now imagine that you have left that suitcase unattended in an airport concourse. It's still a suitcase, your suitcase, but now it's in the wrong place, a suspicious article, possibly dangerous, and no one will take any risks while checking it out. That's how horses feel about everything they see that's not where it should be.

Here are six objects that my horse knows well but when positioned in various places out on a ride she was suspicious of every one of them. However, once she had seen them there once she no longer looked at them twice.

A A striped jump pole across the track.

B A bicycle leaned up against a fence post.

C A flag caught in the hedge.

D A dressage-arena board, something we had worked on that very morning.

E A very scary bag of rubbish.

F And most alarming of all, a feed bucket on the road.

Thinking Like a Human

We are human and although we can try and see the world from a horse's viewpoint, it can be very confusing for us as we watch our horses behave in what seems to be the most illogical fashion at times. Because we can think abstractly, we can often work out a solution to a problem without actually having to do anything physically to try it out. We can put this visualization ability to work and, if employed in a positive way rather than imagining all the disasters that could happen, plan for positive outcomes.

One of my students wanted to ride her horse into a hula hoop and ask him to stop there with his front feet inside it. She was finding this particularly difficult and, after a struggle in which the horse very nimbly kept scooting round the hoop, I made a suggestion.

A I drew two lines straight out from the hoop and told her they were brick walls that she couldn't ride through. On the very next try, she rode straight through the hoop. And on the next attempt, the horse stood quietly with his feet within it.

B I then raked away the brick wall lines and the horse was able to complete the exercise with no problem at all.

There was never a real brick wall but her mind had told her that there was and this had manifested itself to create a positive outcome for her. This is a very powerful ability that humans can put to good use.

The Magic Feather

I am well known in the horse world as having an aversion to whips. I can see no place for them around any animal. What I do see is when people pick up a whip, their energy and their attitude change. They are no longer quiet communicators setting up scenarios in which the horse has time to seek an answer. There is a feeling of hardness, of demanding, of threat. I call whips "Dumbo's Magic Feather."

Dumbo, you may recall, was a really cute baby elephant who did not believe that he could fly. One day he was given a magic feather that he was told held the special magic he needed to fly. Once he was holding the magic feather he was able to take flight by flapping his fabulous ears. But, just when he needed it most, Dumbo lost the feather and, in a terrifying scene, he found himself trapped at the edge of a cliff unable to fly away from the danger bearing down on him.

But his guide implored him, "Fly, Dumbo, for the magic is not in the feather. The magic is within yourself!" And Dumbo flew!

The whip has become like a magic feather. It is time to believe that the magic is not in the whip. Be empowered; the magic is within yourself. That ability to visualize can help you achieve anything you truly want to do.

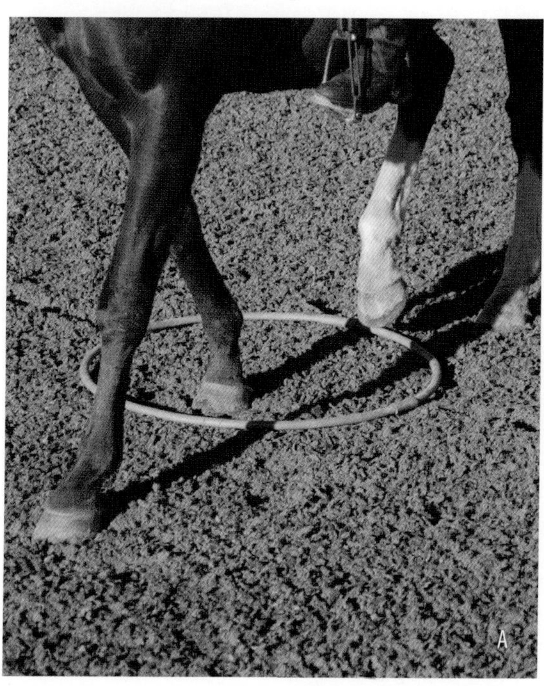
A

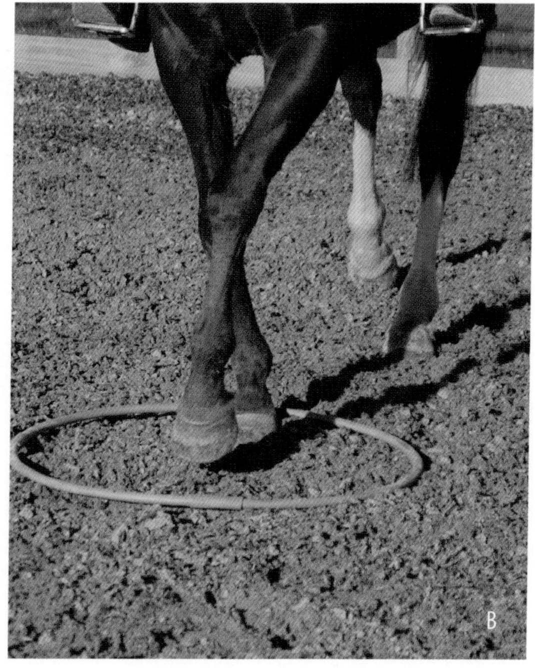
B

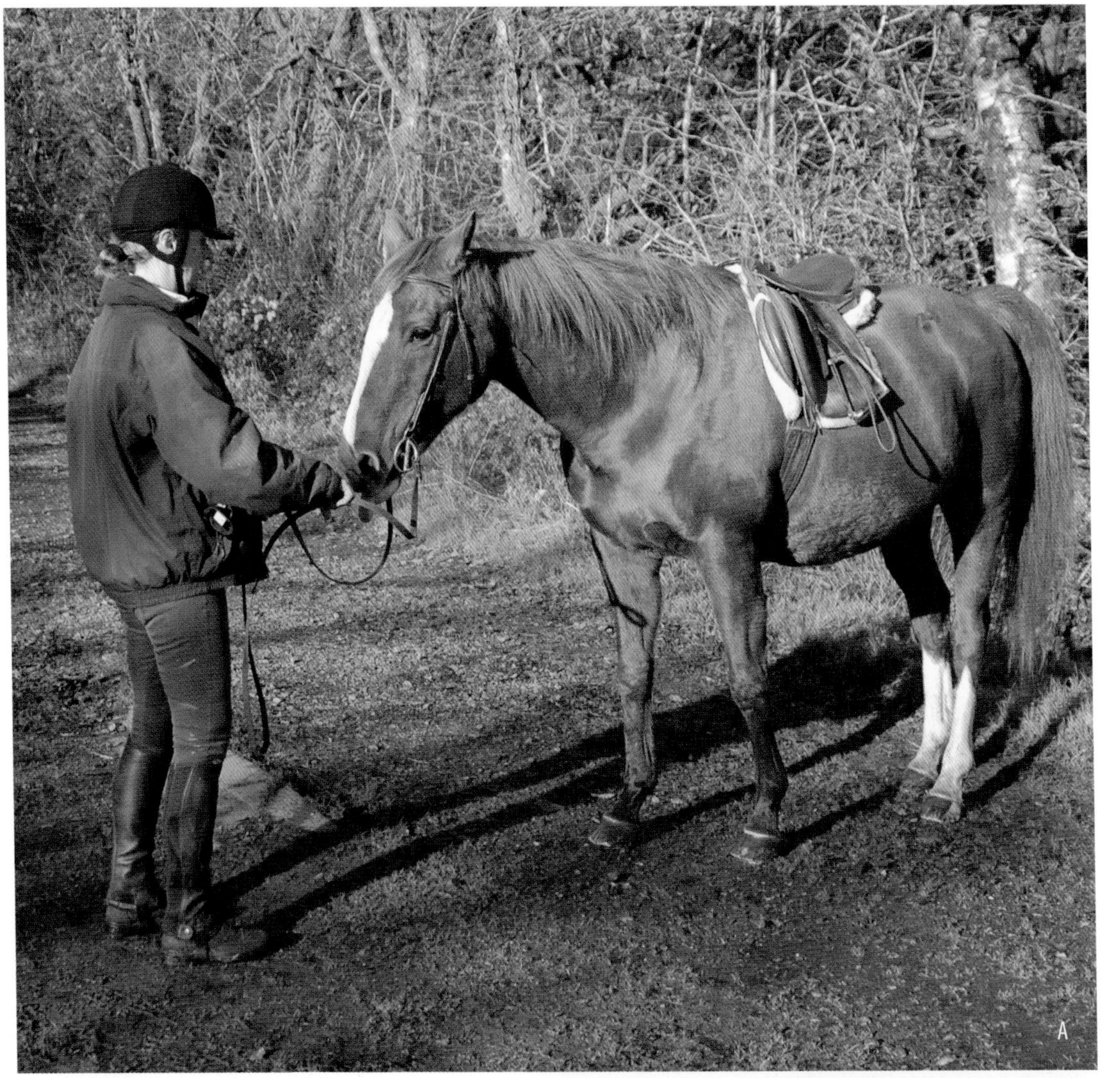

Be a Good Place for Your Horse

There is a very simple exercise that I employ with all my horses and teach to my students because it creates the most amazing results in a horse's ability to keep his attention on you. First of all you need to ensure you are quiet and peaceful within your own self, otherwise the horse will look for peace elsewhere.

A Stand in front of your horse; be still.

B Every time your horse is distracted and looks away, ask him very quietly to bring his face back to you. Do not be harsh; it's just a quiet reminder that he must face you.

C Let your horse know you are a good place to be.

D Your horse will learn to stay still and stand facing you when he finds it is a peaceful place to be.

E When you are in the saddle, carry out exactly the same strategy. Every time the horse looks away from the front you gently bring him back to straight.

F When he is straight sit still and be at peace.

Mini Quiz

How Does Your Horse Show Fear?

1 Observe your horse in a place where he is comfortable with his surroundings and answer the questions in the column "Horse at Peace" in the chart at right.

2 Now, you are going to see what happens when your horse becomes startled. You will need to watch very carefully so that you can really see what is happening. Make a sharp sound, shake a plastic bag or flag, just do something that causes your horse to become slightly scared. You are not terrifying him, just putting him on the alert. Work through the list under "Horse when Afraid," making a note of the changes.

Answer these questions as briefly as you can. Do not make judgments, just write down or draw a rough diagram of what you see:

Observe	Horse at Peace	Horse when Afraid
Eye	Is it round or triangular? Can you see any white or any pink on the lower lid?	Does the eye widen and show a white ring? Does it change its shape?
Ears	Where are they pointing? Backward, out from the side of the head, or flat back? Are they moving?	Do his ears become upright, almost pixie like? Or do they move back against his head? Are they moving?
Nostrils	Soft or flared? Perhaps he blows so the whole nose ripples.	Do his nostrils get larger, does he snort out his breath?
Mouth	Are there wrinkles on the corners? Is the front soft and loose or does it look as though his lips are tight?	Do his lips become more wrinkled, or become very tight, or both?
Neck	What shape is his neck? Where does it bend? At the poll? At the withers or half way down?	Does his neck change shape? Perhaps he has thrown his head up causing his neck to look "upside down."
Belly	Does it look soft and round or tucked up with a "lateral line" running along it from back to front along the edge of his ribs?	Does his belly get smaller and more tucked up?
Tail	Is it clamped down, held to one side or softly hanging? If it is swishing flies, observe how it moves.	Does the tail tuck right in or become raised even to the point where it might bend right over to touch his back?
Feet	Does he graze with one foot forward more often than the others? Does he rest a foot when he is resting?	Are they moving very quickly away from the "scary thing" or do they seem rooted to the ground?

PART ONE: OVER

In this section I am going to introduce obstacles that are predominantly over, which means places where a horse has to travel across something from one side to another.

The color of the ground surface may vary and there may be a change in height. Part of the problem for the horse is that he does not perceive colors as we do or have great depth perception, so deciding whether a color change is, in fact, the shadow of a step up or down is hard for him. In nature, the horse would spend time viewing the obstacle from different angles before he decided how he was going to negotiate it. To start, this investigation might take some time but the more obstacles he encounters and learns about, the quicker he gets at working out how to negotiate them.

The first time my horse met this shallow ditch she clambered through it, but learning from that experience she now knows exactly how to position herself to jump from one side to the other. This skill has been transferred to other ditches, which she jumps safely and willingly (A–D).

Carol is jumping her horse Pearas in hand. Behind you can see the old railway bridge that crosses over the valley (E & F).

1 FORWARD OVER POLES

Walking and trotting over ground rails.

In rides outside the arena you can find yourself crossing all sorts of different terrain, which can be rough with loose rocks or rutted mud baked hard by the sun, or deep sand or snow. When you are riding through forests or woods, there is often a litter of fallen twigs and branches that can pose a hazard to the horse that does not know how to pick up his feet. Even the slightest trip on the part of the horse can unseat the unsteady rider.

Although you ultimately want the horse to be confident enough to pick his own way through this sort of footing, it is worth checking out his ability to do it in the safety of the paddock or the arena. If you have studied the first part of this book you will see that there are plenty of ideas on how to know where the horse's feet are and how you can influence their movement. This first exercise starts to put those principles into practice.

Teaching your horse to calmly walk over poles prepares him for obstacles, such as branches, on the trail.

Exercise 1 • Forward Over Poles

A To stop a pole rolling and scaring your horse, use half-round poles or blocks such as squashed plastic bottles or half-filled sandbags that are safe should the horse step on them.

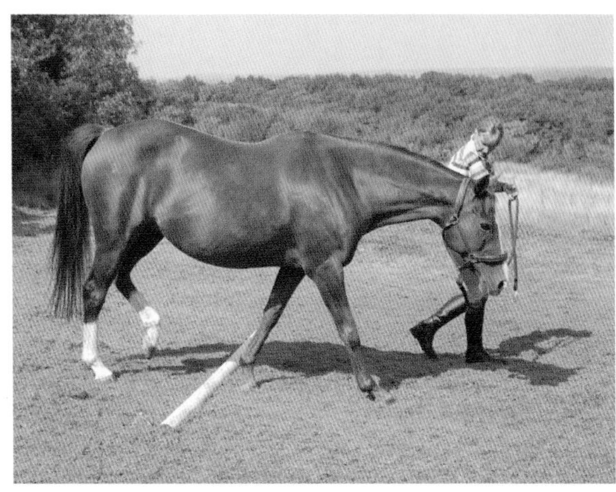

B Start by walking over one pole.

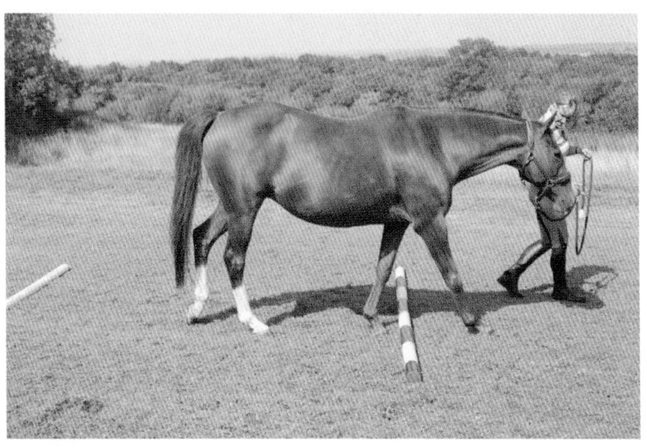

C Then add another, leading the horse on a loose rope and letting him find his own way.

D As you introduce more poles leave between one and two paces between them, depending on the stride of your horse, to make it easier for him when you start trotting.

E Let the horse travel and really think about moving forward over the poles on a loose rope.

F Now pick up the trot; you may want to start with one pole first.

G When you start riding over the poles, keep a loose rein so the horse can find his way.

H Let him look as you ride over but you need to be looking up and forward.

I When you start trotting, keep a loose rein; allow the horse to travel and look up and forward.

J When all is going well you could start to introduce a raised pole, which is the beginning of you and your horse learning to jump.

2 BACKING OVER POLES

Backing over a pole without the horse touching it.

There are going to be times when you need to back your horse with the added challenge of something on the ground that he will need to step over: unloading the trailer, stepping up onto a kerb to avoid vehicles, backing out of a tricky situation in the woods when out on the trail.

Helping your horse understand that this is even possible may seem challenging at first, but I assure you that the rewards of quietly working through this exercise will build mutual trust between you. It will help you understand how your horse feels about reversing into a place that feels blocked, but by listening to your direction he sees that you are aware of his concern and able to help him through it.

As in all these exercises, force has no place here. Quietly setting it up and waiting for the slightest try is the only way you will get a soft result. I suggest you make sure that your horse is comfortable moving forward over poles first by working through the previous exercise before you begin.

When your horse can back quietly over a pole in practice, you will be able to back him over changes in terrain, like the edge of this road, without trouble.

Exercise 2 · Backing Over Poles

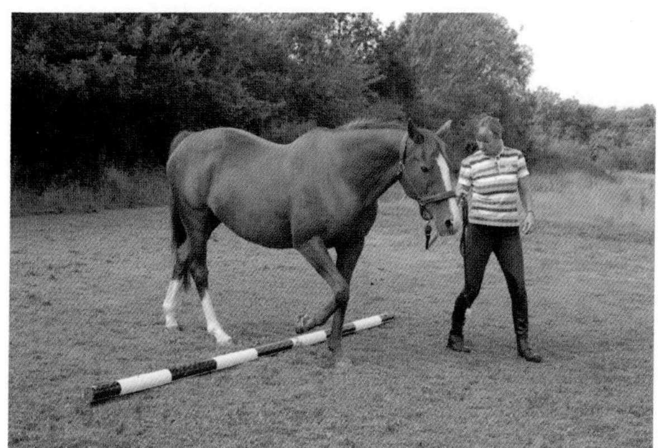

A Make sure your horse is comfortable walking over the pole first.

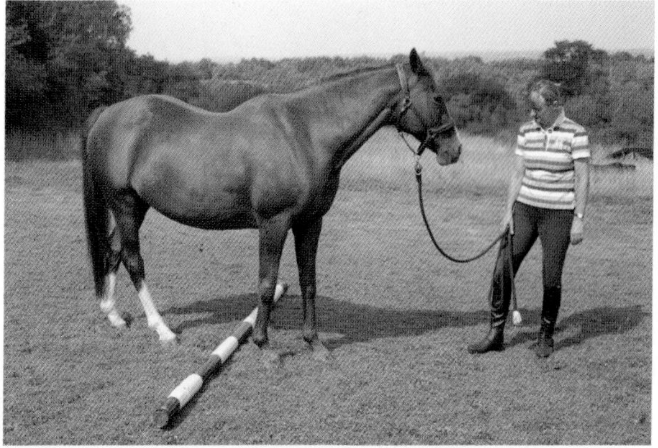

B Lead the horse to the pole and stop halfway over it for one second—or less if this is too long—then walk on slowly. You can increase the time spent standing over the pole as the horse gains confidence.

C Back the horse up over the pole, looking for the moment that the next foot is coming off the ground and lifting the rope and your energy to encourage him to raise that foot higher. You may get your timing wrong however, and, because he didn't lift the foot high enough, he touches the pole. Don't worry, just keep practicing.

D Now you can start leading him until all four feet are over the pole, then halt. Allow him to become comfortable with this before backing up. You can see here Secret is not.

E Next, back your horse, watching for the next foot to come off the ground. As this foot is about to leave the ground, raise your rope and energy.

F When you do this as a ridden exercise, you can get in time with your horse's feet and raise your energy in time with the foot that is about to step over the pole. Here I am in time with Secret's left front foot.

"Sound Advice"

When the Teacher Becomes a Student

A good teacher *shows* his student, he does not tell him, and he is open to new ideas offered by the student.

A student should be attentive, ask questions and offer ideas. If she does not understand, it is not because she is stupid but needs to have the ideas explained in another way.

The student can be a horse or a human.

When you are with your horse, he may question some of your ideas. You should listen: he knows more about being a horse than you do and may have something new to show you.

Allow the student to become the teacher.

3 SIDEWAYS OVER POLES

Sidepassing over poles, cones, and barrels.

Being able to sidepass your horse correctly combines the ability to go forward and backward, move the front end, and move the back end (see *Blueprints 4* and *5* to help you here). A sidepass is the front and back end moving together without any forward or backward so before you start, you are going to isolate each movement and make sure each one works on its own; only then can you start to put them all together.

If you plan to open and close gates when out on the trail, you will need to master all four of these movements. I will show you how later on in the *Through Exercise 4* (p. 126).

Sidepassing over a log will be no problem when you horse can do it over poles or barrels!

Exercise 3 · Sideways Over Poles

A Make sure you can stop your horse and back him up on the ground (see *Blueprint 2* for help, p. 9).

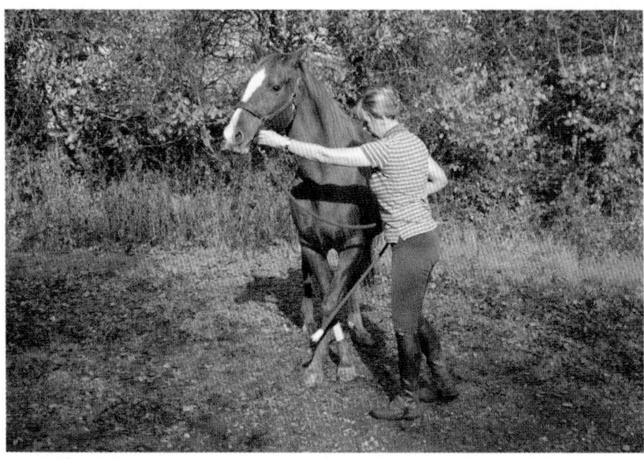

B Check that you can move the front end over easily (see *Blueprint 5*, p. 17).

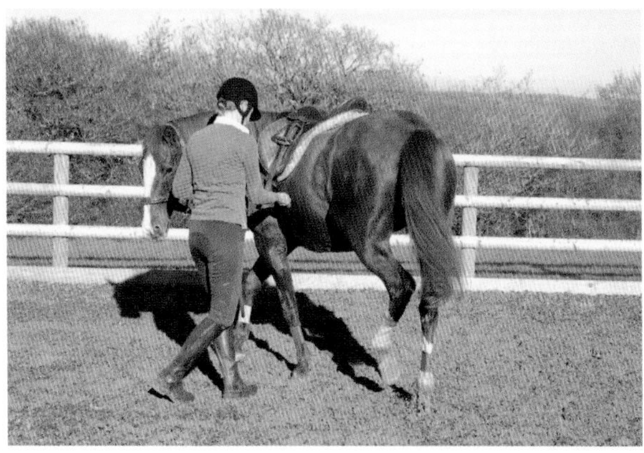

C And make sure that you can move the hind end over (see *Blueprint 4*, p. 14).

D Now move the front and back end over together. If the horse goes forward back him up, if he goes backward, walk him forward.

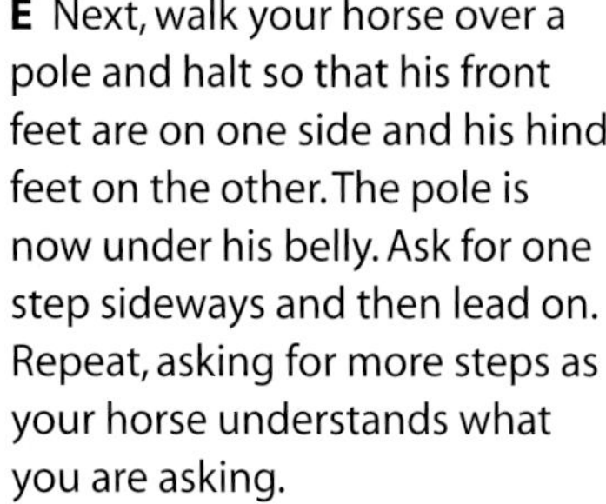

E Next, walk your horse over a pole and halt so that his front feet are on one side and his hind feet on the other. The pole is now under his belly. Ask for one step sideways and then lead on. Repeat, asking for more steps as your horse understands what you are asking.

F You are ready to start right at the end of a pole and move along.

G Introduce a safe item and pass over it.

H Slowly increase the size of the object.

I Ride over a pole and halt; ask the front end to move over. If you find this difficult then check *Blueprint 5* for help.

J Now move the back end over; check *Blueprint 4* for help here.

Exercise 3 · Sideways Over Poles (cont.)

K Now move them at the same time.

L Sidepass over a cone; this is the front end.

M Sidepass over a cone; this is the back end.

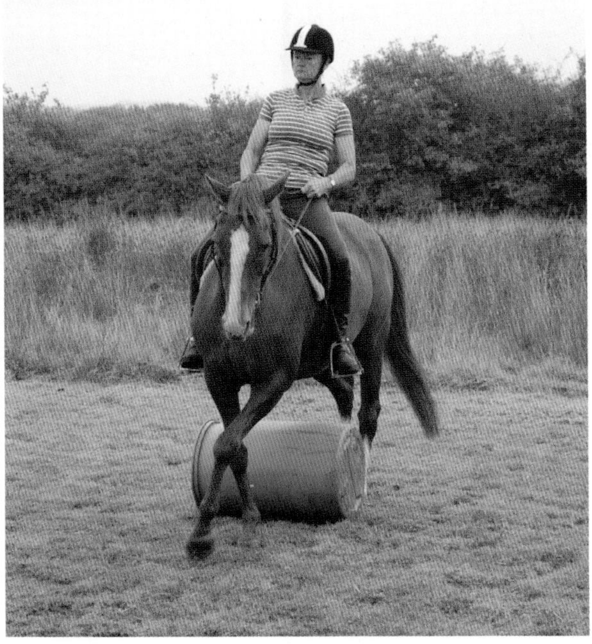

N Sidepass over a barrel.

4 WHITE LINES

Crossing white objects and street markings.

Whenever we take our horses out on a public road we have a duty of care to other users. You cannot be 100 percent sure that your horse will not spook at an unforeseen event, but white lines on the road are not in that category. Some new white lines and wording were painted onto the road through our village and my horse Secret made it quite plain that these brand new sparkling white lines were a definite trap. It seemed an ideal training opportunity and you can see in the photos how I got on. Because I believe in solid groundwork I was able to confidently dismount, and despite not having my halter and long lead rope, I was able to show Secret that the white lines were quite safe. I then remounted and was able to walk over them without any fear at all.

White road markings come in all shapes and sizes.

Exercise 4 · White Lines

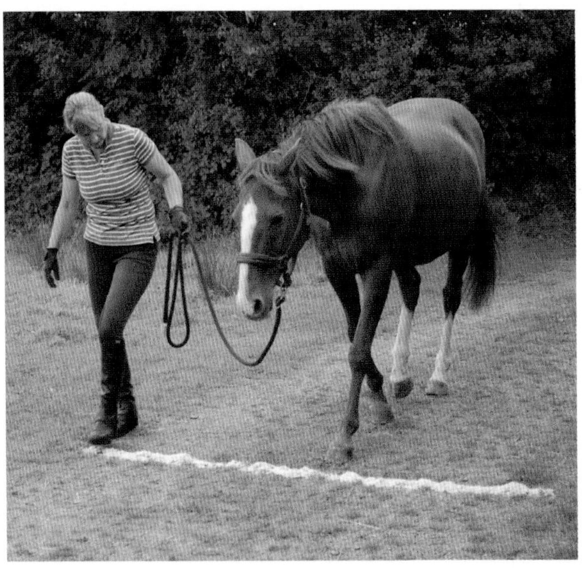

A Start with sawdust or shavings and make a thin line on the ground.

B Introduce more lines of shavings.

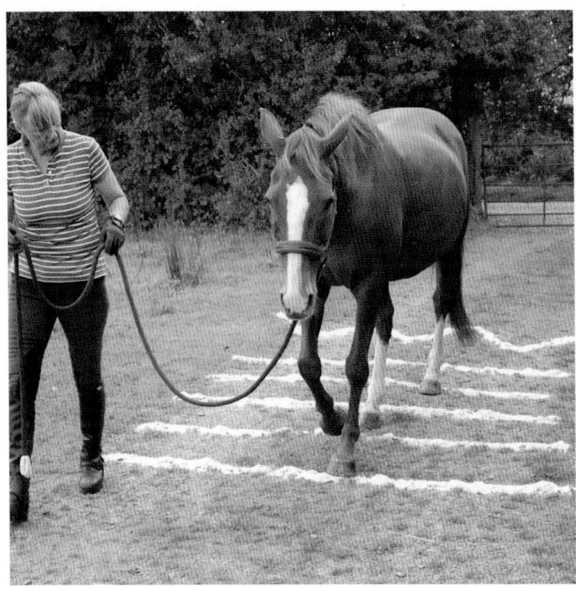

C Keep adding lines until you have a striped effect for the horse to walk over.

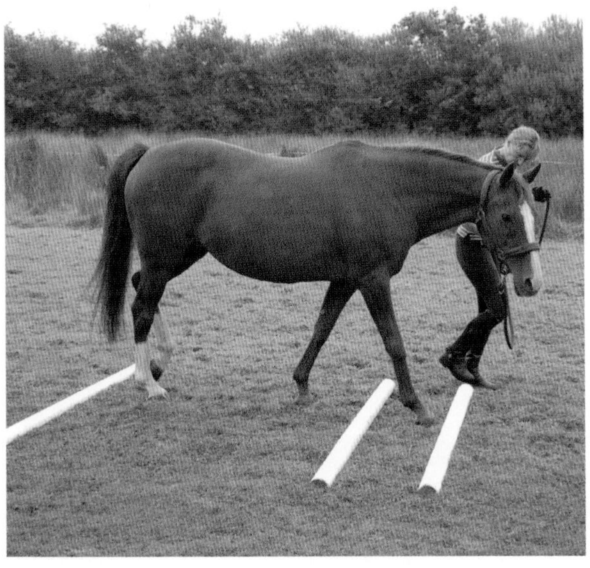

D If you cannot get shavings you can use white painted poles.

E Now ride over your sawdust lines.

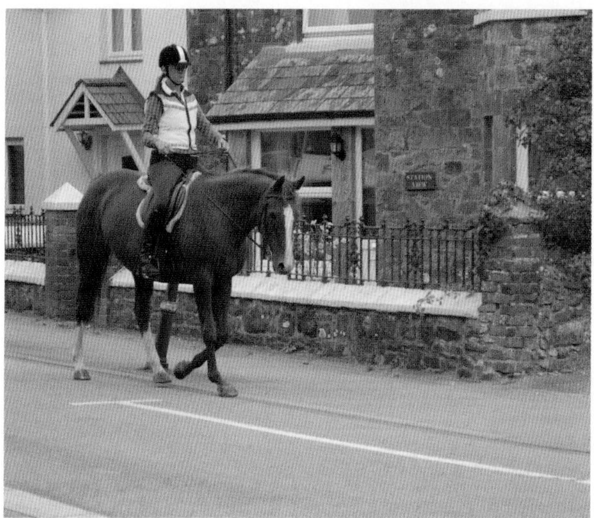

F On a ride, a single line may attract attention.

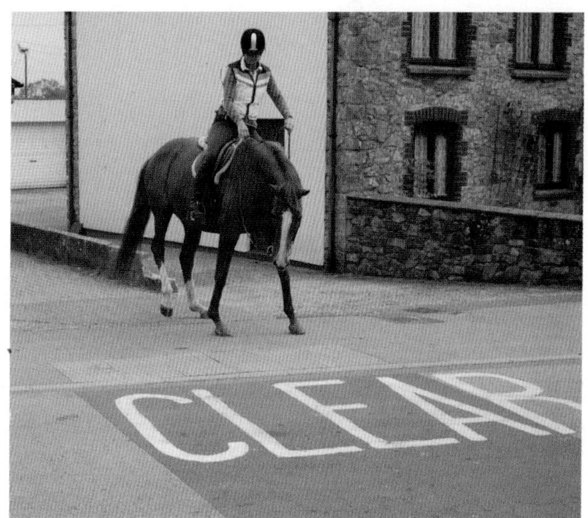

G Whole words get a much bigger reaction.

Exercise 4 · White Lines (cont.)

H If your ground skills are good then you can get off and show him it is safe.

I When you get back he will probably be a lot more comfortable, but give him time to look.

J Very soon he will realize they are safe and he will stand on them.

OVER

5 THRESHOLDS

Experiencing footing changes and step-overs.

A threshold is any change in surface where there is a definite line between the two. It was wild ponies that taught me about thresholds. The thing about handling untouched ponies is that they are a "clean slate" and question everything they are unsure about, either by being quietly suspicious, dramatically fearful, or anywhere in between.

When we had them haltered and set about teaching them to lead, the first thing they taught me was how to move each individual foot, and secondly, that any change in surface, be it from wet to dry, earth to straw, or stone to concrete, needed careful inspection before a step was made.

I then began to notice it in domestic horses. Often, people would complain that their horse didn't like getting muddy feet, or didn't want to leave his stall, or step up onto a ramp, but then I began to see that the horse was often inspecting the floor and the change from one type of surface to another. By blurring that sudden difference—spreading straw, earth, or shavings to soften the edge—the horse would often step over. It was as if the sharply defined edge was something to be suspicious of, or perhaps, with horses not having a perception of depth, they didn't know how far to step up or down. I have found that the more you do this, the more confident horses become.

Your horse can learn to confidently step from one distinct surface, or change in footing, to another.

Exercise 5 · Thresholds

A Here we have a wet edge and a dry center; the shadow is forming a threshold, too.

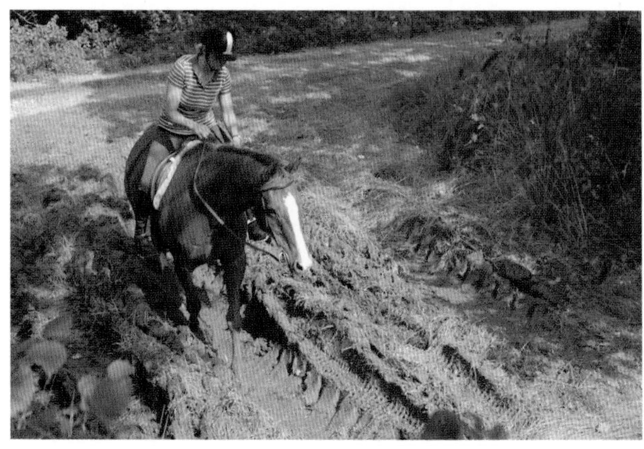

B Here the shadow is much more obvious.

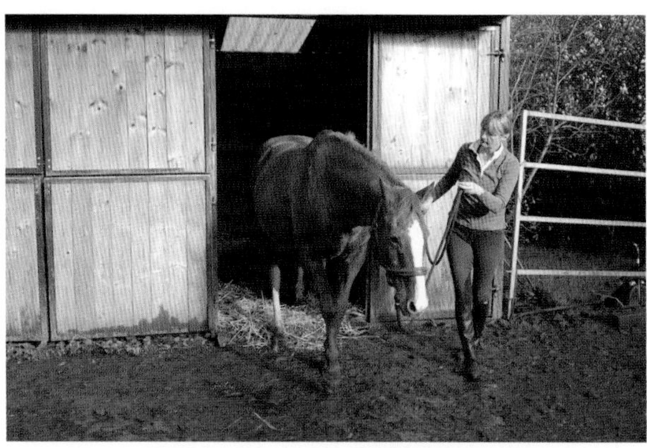

C A step over into or out of a stall is one of the commonest thresholds for wild ponies to negotiate on their first lead out.

D Even a simple hosepipe can cause a horse to stop and look.

E A new heap of bark peelings provides a new threshold to play on. Here, I am asking my horse to step from the grass onto the bark. I ask and wait.

F Let your horse look at the change in surface—you can see here the horse is checking out the threshold.

G When he crosses the threshold, allow him to travel.

H Here the threshold is a change from tarmac to special paving slabs that mark a human road-crossing place. Let the horse look by giving the reins to him.

I If that isn't enough, you could get off and show him.

J Now let him look as you ride.

K Very soon, with your help, he will understand that it is safe to step over the edge.

Side Story

The Arab Horse and the Hula Hoop

When I was in Canada I met an Arabian that really showed me how astute the equine race can be. This little Arab had been quite unable to step into the closed hula hoop so we opened it and worked through stepping into the hoop, gradually closing it up until there was only a tiny gap about a quarter-inch or half-a-centimeter wide.

Deciding it was as good as closed, with the horse looking very relaxed about stepping in and standing still, we closed up the hoop. Immediately the horse said, "No." He told us quite plainly that the hoop was now a closed space and there was absolutely no way he was stepping into it. We opened the hoop half-an-inch again and he happily walked in and stood still.

Eventually, he did gain enough confidence to step in and realize that he was safe. That tiny gap made all the difference to him. It made me realize that the horse is seeing things in much greater detail than we do and we need to look at the world with precision if we are to become successful in our interactions with horses.

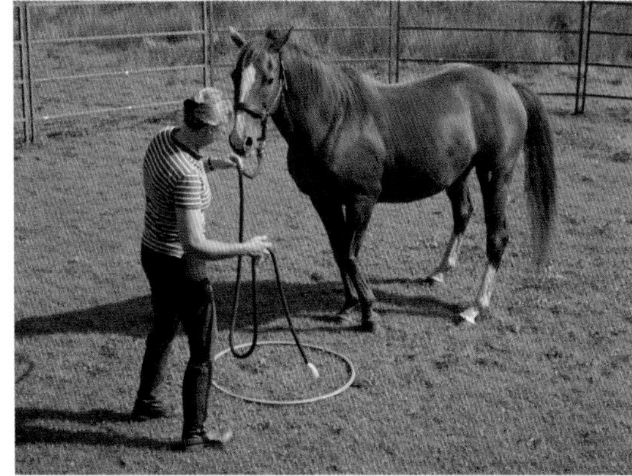

A You can see the horse is braced behind and not happy about stepping into the hoop.

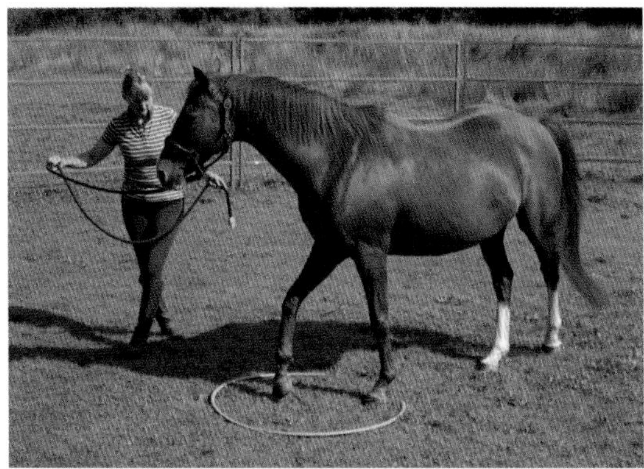

B I open the hoop and allow him to get used to the open hoop before I slowly close it.

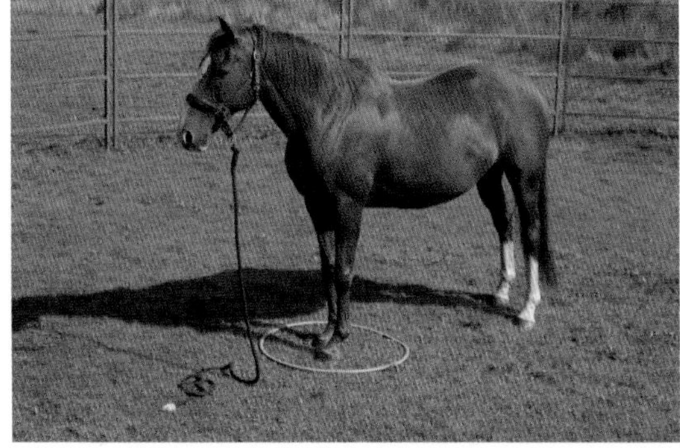

C It takes hardly any time for the horse to realize it is quite safe to step into the hoop and stand still.

6 HULA HOOPS

Stepping into a hula hoop and standing still.

I have been enormously fortunate to have traveled extensively teaching the sport of Horse Agility to thousands of horses and their people. When I first invented the sport I wanted to design easy obstacles for our Starter competitors and decided that asking a horse to step into a hula hoop lying on the ground would be an easy start.

Very soon I found it was not as easy as I had thought. A hula hoop is a closed space—it has an inside and an outside—and as I worked, I saw that many horses did not want to step into that closed hoop. To us humans, it was obvious it was a piece of pipe lying on the ground and that the inside surface was the same as the outside, but to the horse, this plainly was not the case. In fact the Hula Hoop obstacle has caused many a wail of despair as people try and encourage their horse to step in and stand still. I really had to think about how I could make this easier for people and their horses, and here's the result. This is an exercise in trust and foot-placing.

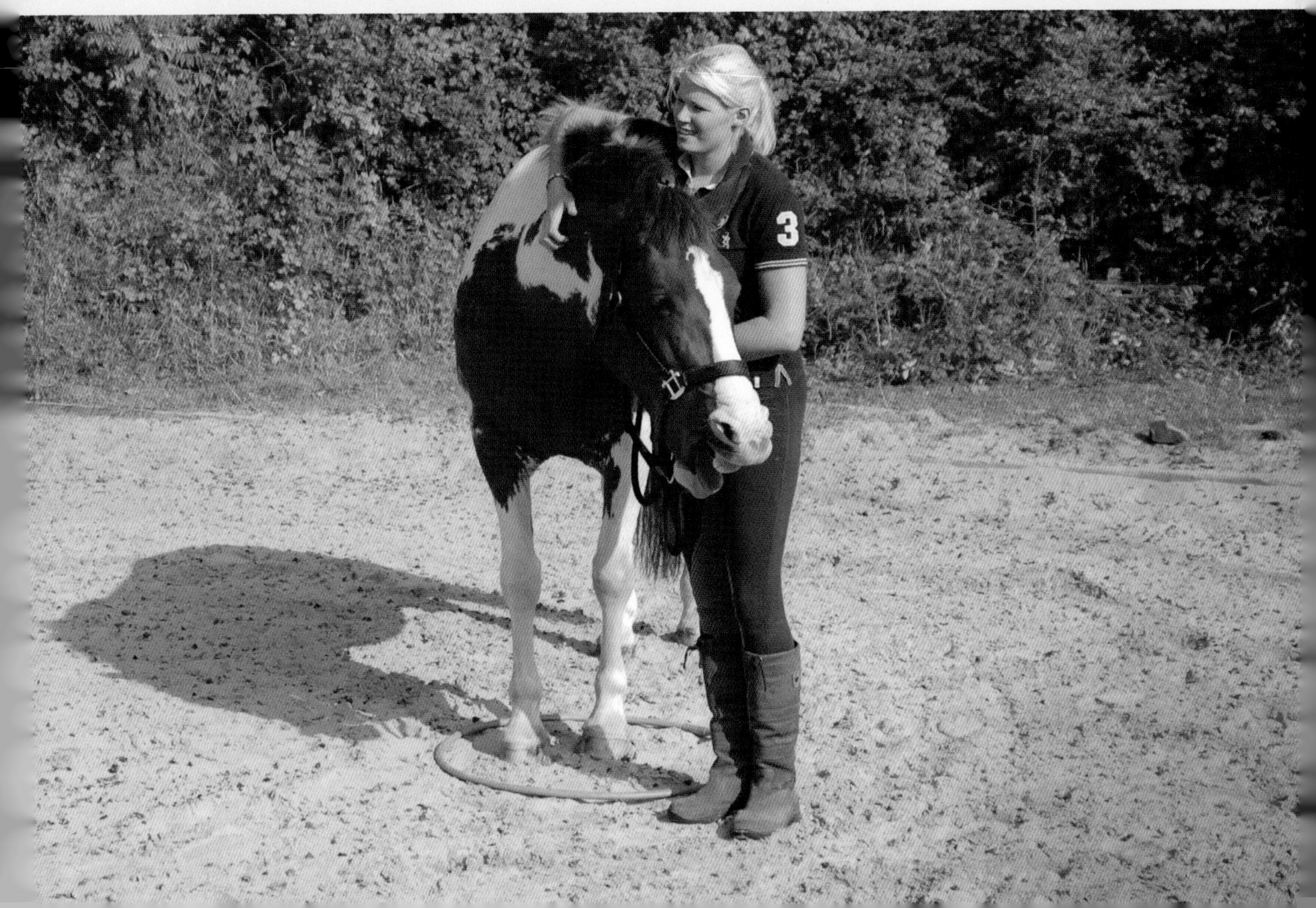

Standing within the hula hoop is an exercise in trust-building and control of the horse's feet.

Exercise 6 · Hula Hoops

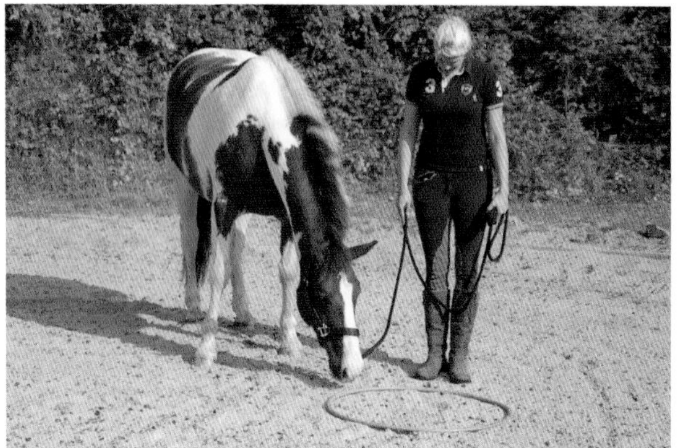

A Let the horse look.

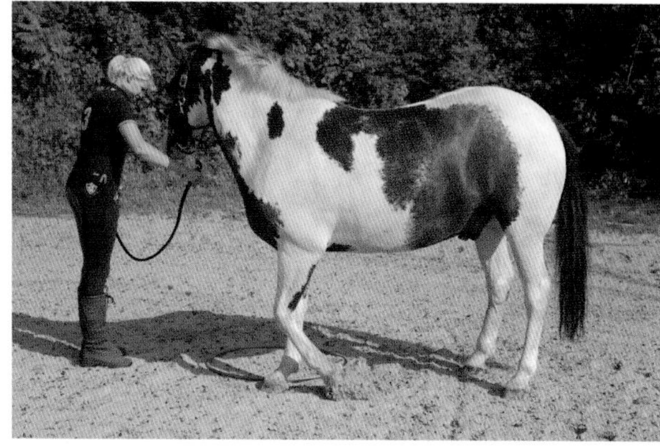

B Many horses do not like to put their feet into the closed circle.

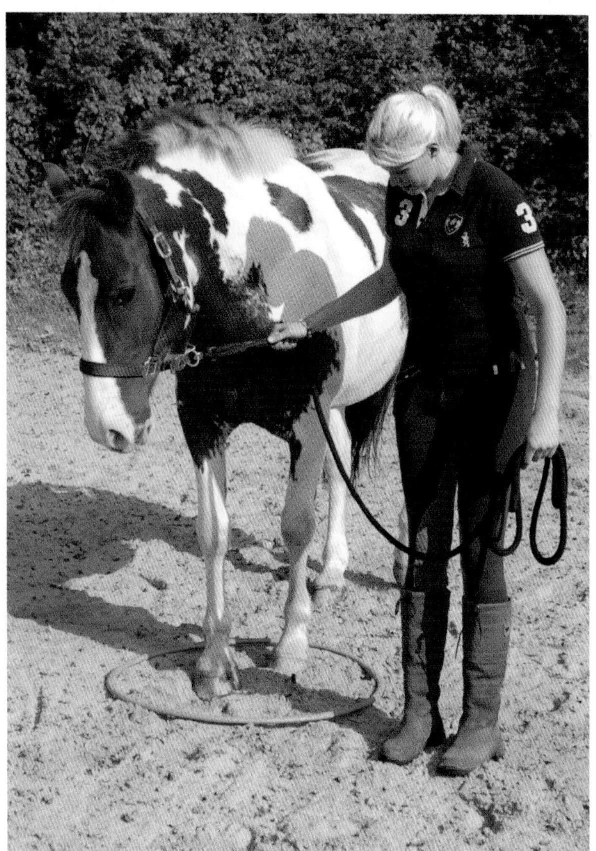

C This horse is not happy.

D He steps out with one foot because he feels safer that way.

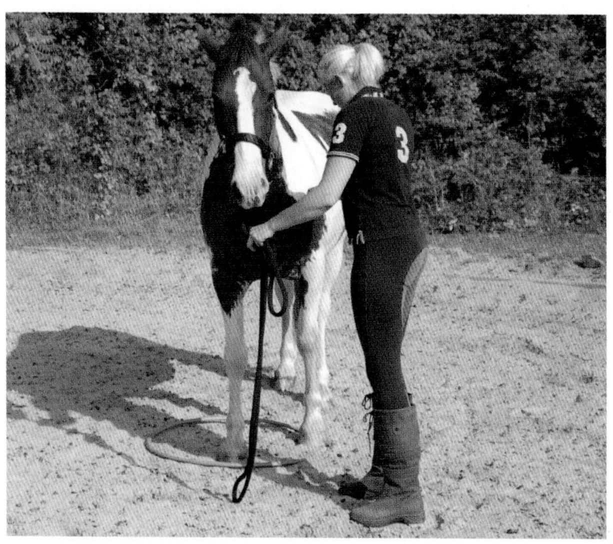

E Some horses keep one foot on the edge.

F We always use a hula hoop that will break open if the horse gets his feet caught so now we can open up the hoop and lead the horse through.

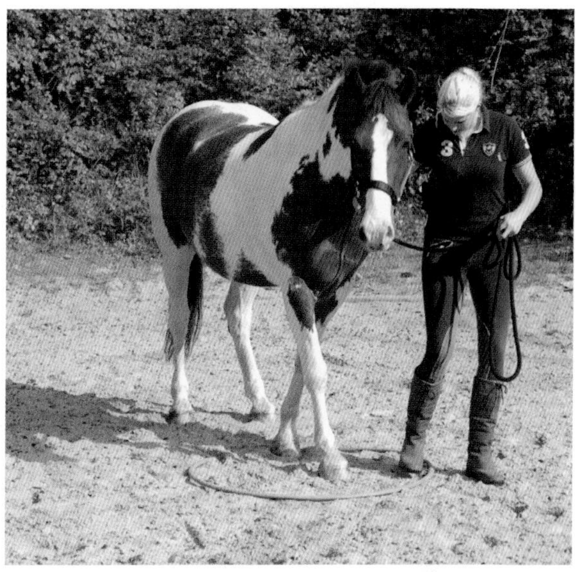

G When the horse is comfortable walking through, stop in the hoop with his front feet for one second, then lead on.

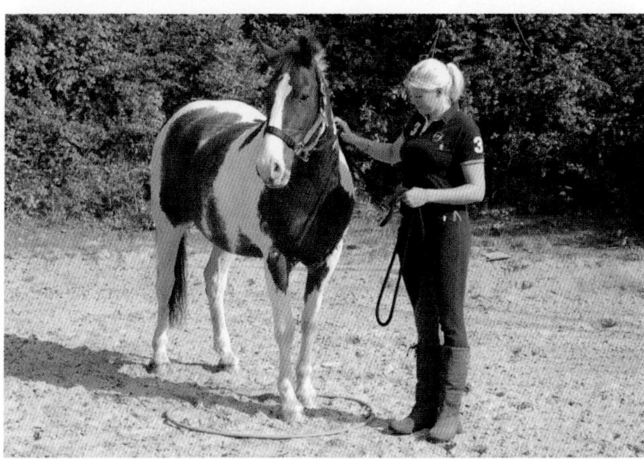

H As he settles to the task, increase the time of the stop.

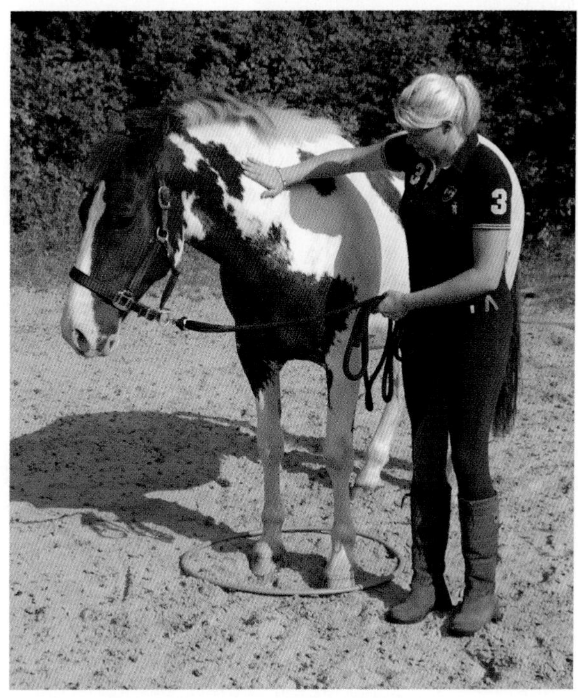

J Eventually you will be able to walk him into the hoop and he will stand still.

I When he is happy, slowly repeat the exercise, closing the hoop up a little at a time.

7 TARPAULINS

Crossing surfaces like tarps, carpets and rubber mats.

Although we have used a tarpaulin in this exercise, you can use any safe flat surface to practice this exercise. The more varied the surfaces become in texture, color, and size, the more a horse will trust in you when you say a surface is safe to cross. Different types of tarpaulins, old carpets, and rubber mats are all useful here. Make sure they are not slippery when wet or dry or that the fabric has not split or shredded; a horse could catch his feet thus "attaching" himself to the fabric, which may cause panic as it drags along at his feet.

The more you walk your horse over different surfaces, the more confident he will become.

The more you walk your horse over different surfaces the more confident he will become.

Exercise 7 · Tarpaulins

A Choose a tarpaulin or heavy fabric that will not shred or get wrapped around the horse's feet, and let the horse look.

B If the horse really cannot step on it, you can try using two tarpaulins and set them at an angle to each other with a small gap between them. Let the horse become happy walking through this gap.

C Now slowly close the gap. Sometimes you may only be able to move them together by an inch or two; don't rush—let the horse explore this new surface.

D Eventually, you will be able to overlap the tarpaulins and the horse will step onto them—even if only with one foot. There is no rush; many horses find this very frightening.

E If your ground skills are solid and your horse knows not to push into your personal space, you can send him over from the side. You could start with a gap between the tarpaulin and the fence, making the gap narrower as he becomes more comfortable with the proximity of the new surface.

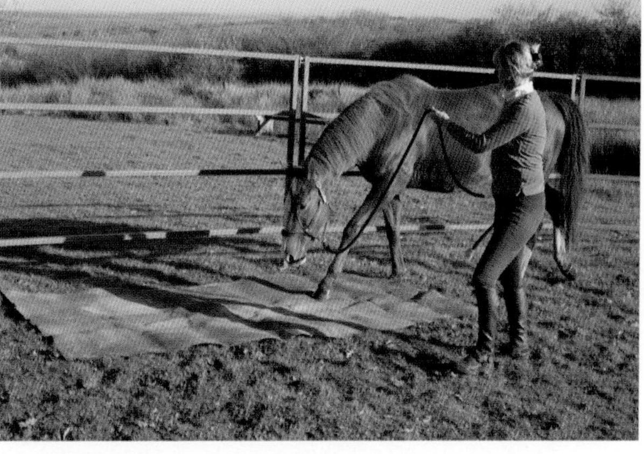

F Change the surface once your horse finds one type easy. The more experiences you give him the safer he will become.

8 DARK AND LIGHT

Going from bright light into shadows or dark areas.

We all know horses see the world in a different way to humans. I could write a long piece about the rods and cones (those are the special cells in the eyes that see color and black and white), but really all we need to know is horses find moving from bright light into shadow, and vice versa, more difficult than we do because it takes longer for their eyes to adjust to the sudden change.

When you think how well horses can see at night you may realize they would never need to adjust quickly from darkness to daylight in the wild. It's a skill they've never had to develop. I feel that for a horse with a rider to move confidently through these different light intensities requires a great deal of trust. Jumping from bright sunlight into dark woodland, as happens on some cross-country courses, must take some courage if you suddenly can't see where you're going.

When you have a shadow and a very uneven surface, as seen in the photo on this page, give your horse his head so he can work out how to safely cross.

As we cross a shadow and a very uneven surface, I give Secret her head so she can work out how to safely cross.

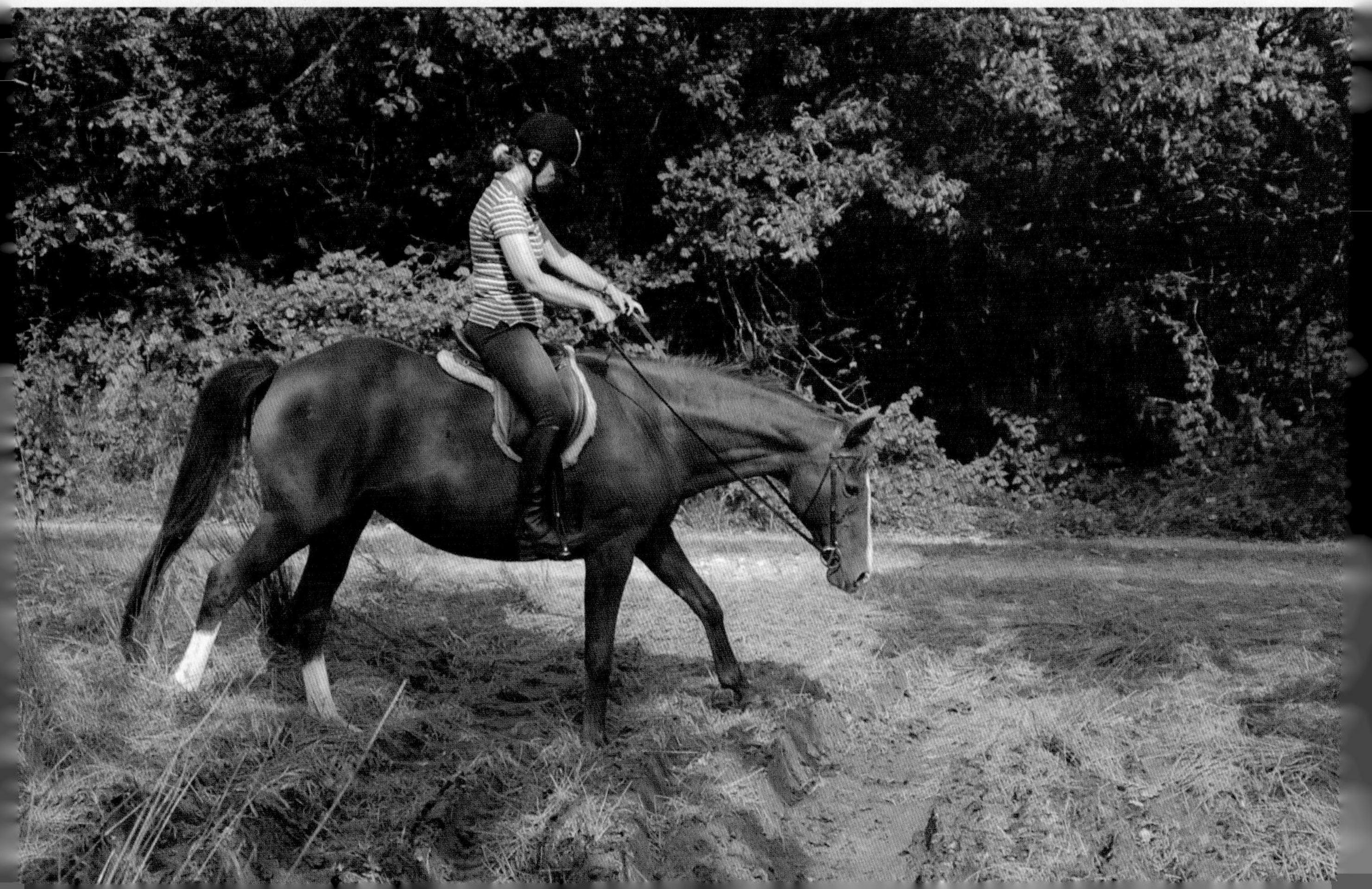

Exercise 8 · Dark and Light

A The best way to start here is on the flat gently moving through different intensities of shadow while guiding your horse.

B This horse has cantered from bright sun into shadow but can see the brighter area ahead so feels confident to travel forward.

C This is a different story. The photo gives us a good idea of how dark this must appear to a horse.

D To humans the change from bright to dark doesn't look that dramatic when we look into the wood, but in the previous photo, the camera helps you appreciate what the horse can see.

E Here we have a change in height with the added challenge of deep shadow.

F You can see how the horse is less forward-going at this step down but the rider lets the reins slip a little, looks up, and lets the horse find his way without interference.

9 ROAD FURNITURE

Accepting objects on and along roads, from drain covers to signposts.

The last thing you need when traveling along the road is a horse shying into it to avoid something as mundane as a drain cover or other roadside fitting. These items are all pretty similar in their design so there is every opportunity to help your horse become so familiar with them that he does not feel the need to escape.

If you are already in a situation where a horse is looking to spook, the worst thing to do is "growl" at him and tell him off. That is exactly what he thinks is going to happen as the drain cover leaps out to chase him. Reassure him and, when safe, dismount; by making friends with the perceived monster, he will often see that it is not so scary after all. Even better, get really good on the ground with your horse and go for walks to show him the sights that he will encounter when out and about, and very soon he will learn to ignore them.

Road signs, automobiles, street lights—oh my!

Exercise 9 · Road Furniture

A A simple ride through the village has many items of interest to a horse.

B A drain cover catches the horse's eye; there's an inspection cover on the other side too, and we have to ride between them.

C With any new object, if possible let the horse inspect it. Use *Advance and Retreat* methods (*Blueprint 3*, p. 11) if you need to help your horse here.

D After my horse has inspected a new object I do not focus on it but ride forward and look where I actually want to go.

E With tricky objects, like this salt box, make these places where you stop and have a rest.

F Long ago I would have avoided this roadside hazard; now I make special trips just to see how I can work with my horse to help her become comfortable with them.

Side Story

Why Stand on a Podium?

Horse owners who play over obstacles with their horses, especially without riding them, are often told they are just "doing tricks." I wondered what the difference was between a "trick" and a "skill" so I did a bit of research on the subject.

It appears that a skill is something an animal does that is useful to the human training him. For example, a horse walking up a ramp into a truck is a useful skill for people who want to move their horses from one place to another in a truck.

A trick, however, is defined as an unnatural act performed purely for entertainment with no value to the human training the horse. So the horse standing on a podium appears to be a trick because the act of stepping up onto an isolated raised surface does not appear to have a practical use. But supposing you ran a circus, and people paid to see this trick, does it then become a skill?

If you look at the podium as a "training obstacle," without worrying about whether the act of teaching a horse to step up onto it is a trick or a skill, you can begin to see relationships between this action and other things you may want the horse to do.

If you look at the photo sequence here, you can see how the trick of standing my horse on a podium and teaching her to walk over an agility A Frame obstacle has a practical purpose. It's given her the skills needed to walk up a ramp and stand on a flat raised surface. Little imagination is needed to see how these two tricks have made my horse extremely skillful at loading into a van whenever I ask her.

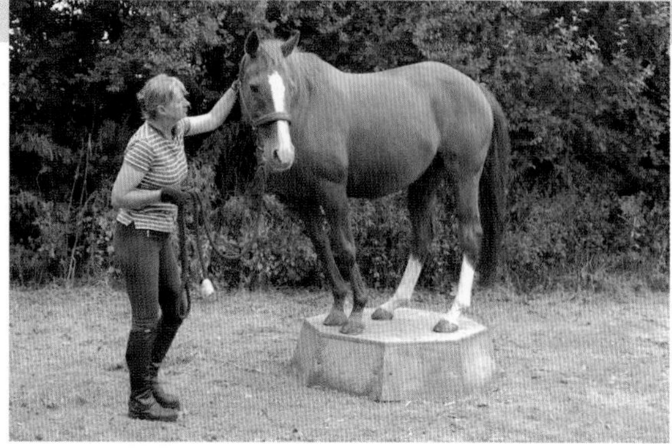

A After a quick inspection my horse had no hesitation about standing on this podium even though she had never seen it before.

B This is just a big podium with ramps going up to it.

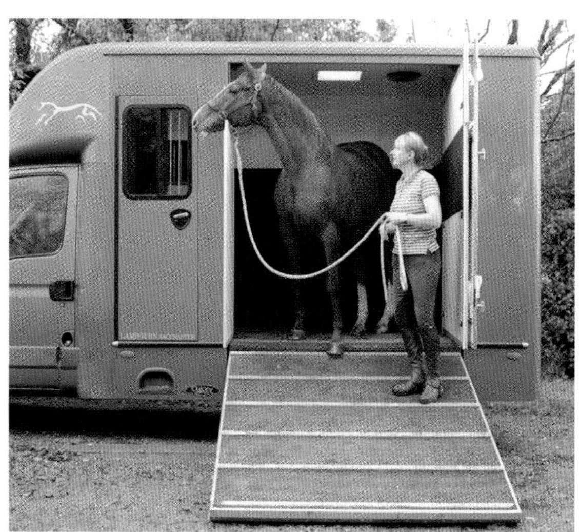

C Here we have a podium with a ramp going up to it; this one has wheels as well.

10 PODIUMS

Stepping onto a podium.

This is the one obstacle that gets regularly labeled as a "circus trick" but how wrong people are in their labeling of this interesting obstacle. How many times would you like your horse to jump up or down steps on a cross country course? Do you ever want your horse to step up into a trailer or even jump up into a truck? Even if you cannot foresee these events, giving you and your horse as many training opportunities as possible can only strengthen your trust in each other, so why not? I'm all for having fun with my horse and if I see something that will be an interesting challenge for us both then I'm up for it.

Secret at home on the podium.

Exercise 10 · Podiums

A This is a purpose-made podium.

B A tire filled with gravel and soil as part of our agility bridge.

C Start with a low podium, if possible, and allow the horse to look.

D He may need to paw.

E Be content with one foot to start.

F You can lift one foot onto it to encourage him.

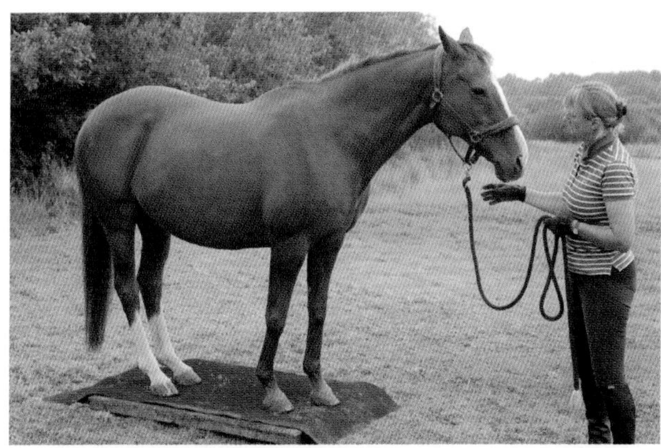

G Eventually you will get all four feet on but don't hurry, let him find his way.

H Moving to a higher podium, we start at the beginning by letting him look.

I Let him paw and explore the new surface.

J First the front feet step up; now wait for him to work out how to get his back feet on.

K Be patient and let him feel his way with the back feet.

11 BRIDGES

Crossing a bridge and a teeter-totter (seesaw).

Bridges come in all shapes and sizes from plank bridges across the rivers to wide bridges over highways with fast vehicles whizzing along them. At some point on your rides out you may need to go across a bridge if you want to continue on the trail; otherwise you might need to make a big detour or just turn around and head home.

Always ensure a bridge has been designed with horses in mind; a small bridge built to carry people may be too weak, or even too slippery for a horse, and on some bridges it is safer to dismount and lead your horse over. So we come back to solid ground skills again!

With proper preparation, going over a bridge is just another stride down the trail.

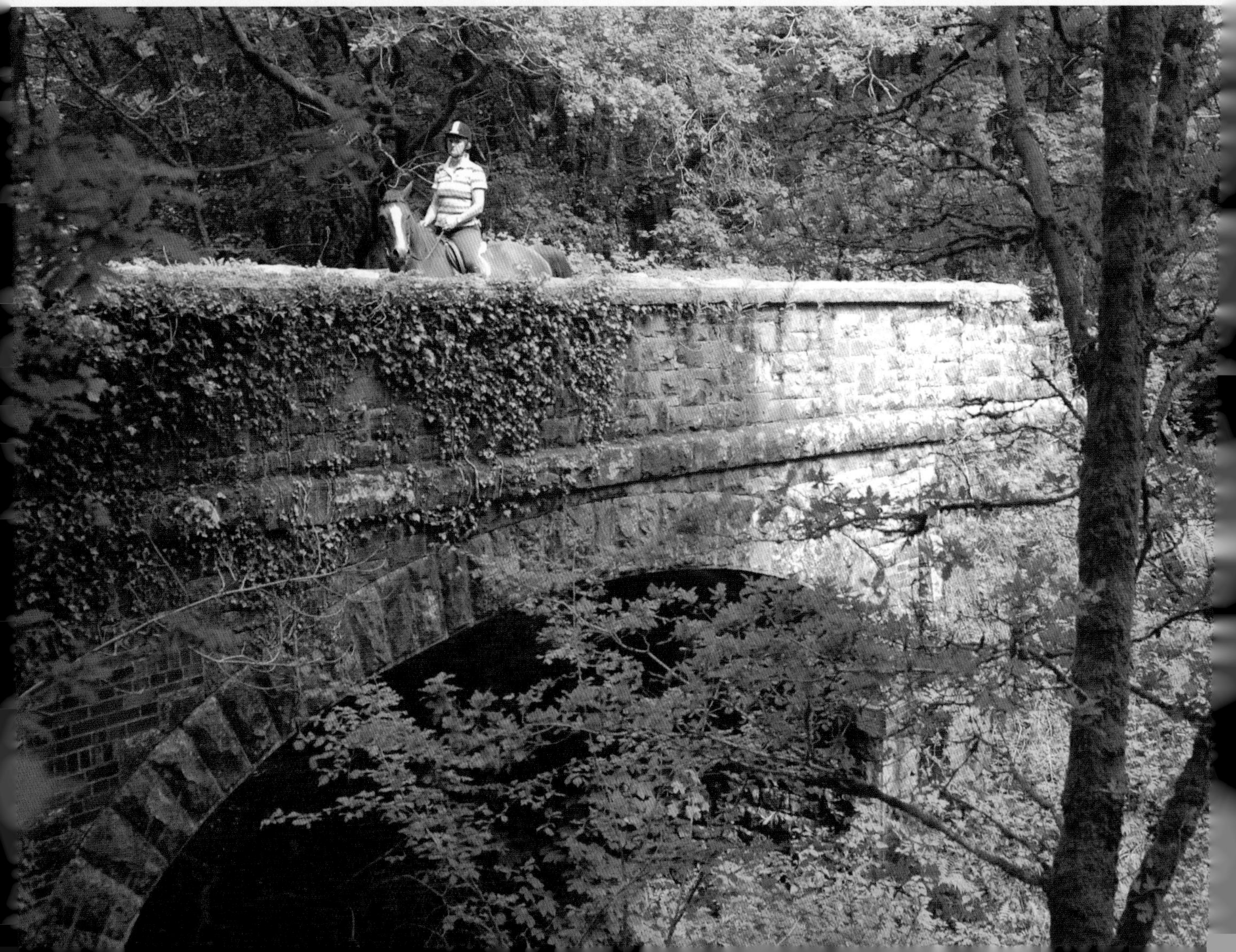

Exercise 11 · Bridges

A Make sure the horse can walk over a tarpaulin first.

B Then offer the flat bridge. If walking along it is too much, try going from side to side. The horse may step right over but as he gains confidence you will see that he starts to drop the odd foot onto the surface as he steps across.

C Don't try and stop him exploring; let him look, smell, and paw the surface if he needs to.

D Now put a small pivot in the middle. This one may be too big to start with: you could just use a small pebble or broom handle to get a tiny movement to begin.

E Keep out of the way when the teeter-totter drops down as your horse may take fright and jump off.

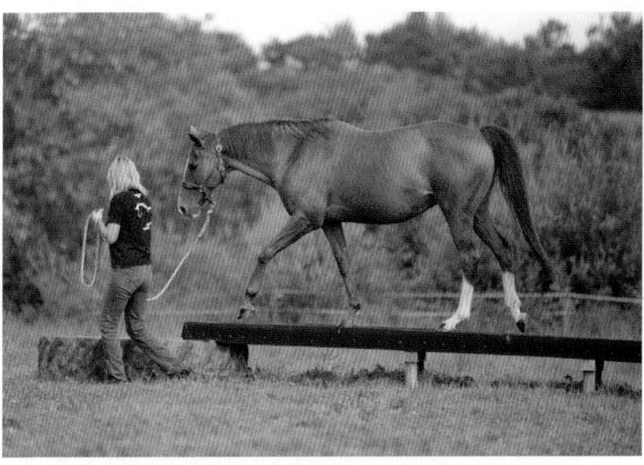

F This is our full-size agility bridge. Once the horses have been allowed to explore how it smells and sounds, they are very comfortable as they cross it.

"Sound Advice"

A Stand on a flat surface and balance your weight evenly through each foot.

B Look down at your right foot.

C Now lift your right foot off the ground; how easy does it feel?

D Now stand up again and balance your weight evenly through both feet.

E Look up to the right.

F Now lift your foot. Much easier, isn't it?

Eyes Are Heavy

Many of us have a habit of looking down while we are riding. We look at the ears of our horse, the ground, or we lean over to see if we are getting it right when learning to move individual feet. Try the following experiment and I think you'll begin to appreciate how difficult we are making it for our horse to move.

If you were riding your horse and asking him to lift his right front foot off the ground, imagine how difficult it must be if you suddenly lean over and peer down to see if it is working. So look up and feel that foot lifting; it'll be so much easier for both of you.

12 RAMPS

Walking up and down steep ramps and slopes.

One of the first horse-agility obstacles we built at home was a big A-frame with a square platform on top. It was a very interesting way of learning to direct the horse's feet up a fairly steep ramp and down the other side without him feeling he needed to leap off halfway over.

A journalist came to write a piece for a magazine and asked why on earth you would want to do that with your horse. Of course, with all my obstacles, they are either there to put principles to purpose or have a connection to a real-life task. I replied with a question: "Have you never loaded your horse into a trailer?" She looked a bit embarrassed but had the grace to look around the obstacle course and say, "Now I see, they all mean something, don't they?"

Yes, they do, but if it's only to build a trusting relationship between you and your horse, then that's good enough for me.

By teaching your horse to navigate up and down ramps in hand, he will be prepared when faced with steep banks like this one.

Exercise 12 · Ramps

A Make sure the horse can cross a tarp first.

B Using a podium or bridge to show him how to step up is very useful.

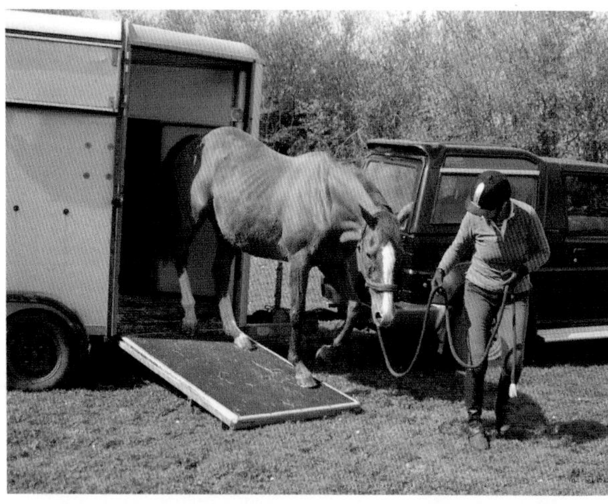

C A trailer ramp is a good start. Use a long rope so the horse has room to move.

D Some horses can happily put their front feet onto the ramp but not the back.

E On a ramp that is less steep, you can walk over it from side to side.

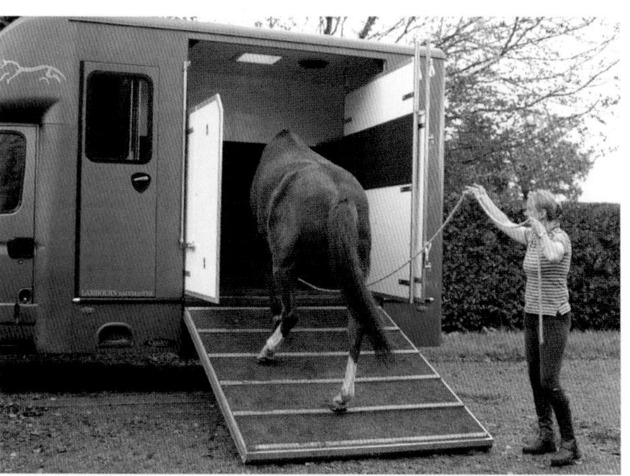

F This helps a horse load with confidence onto a van.

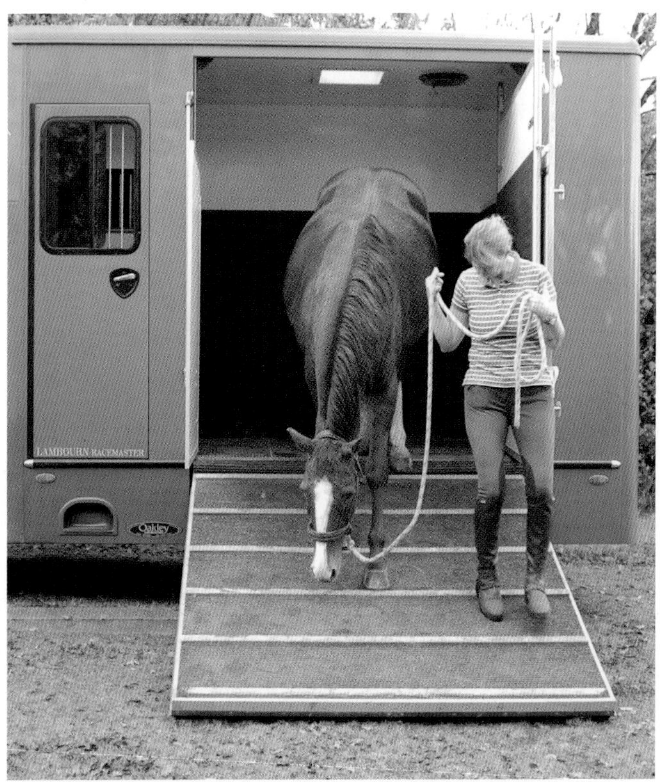

G ...and unload.

H It's an easy step to encourage him to go up onto a horse-agility obstacle...

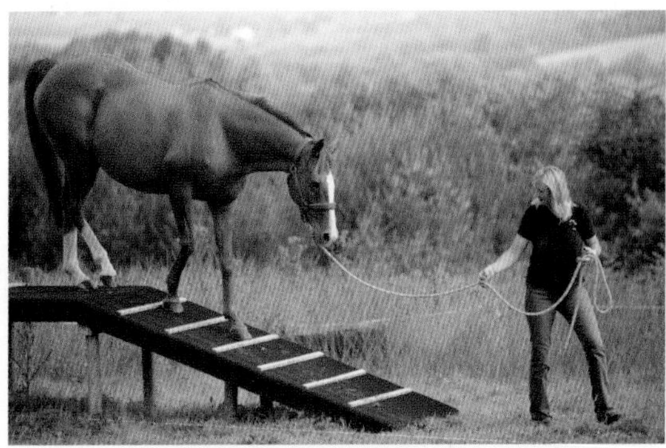

I ...and come down the other side.

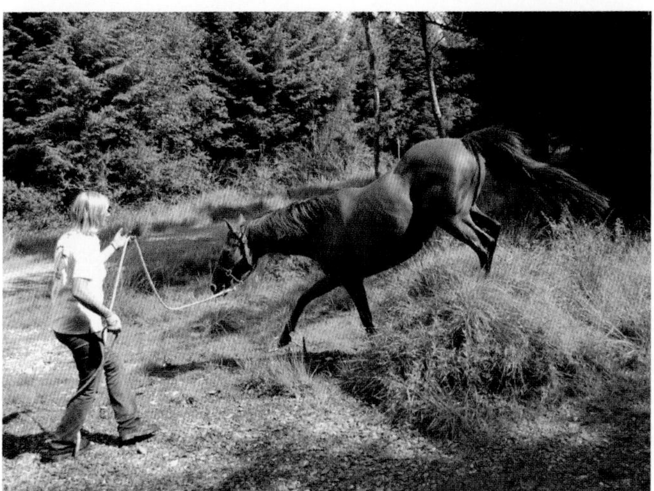

J Let the horse explore different ways of tackling steep ramps without the weight of a rider.

K Then take opportunities to let him explore with a rider on board. Keep the ramps shallow and short to start.

13 STEPS

Negotiating flights of steps and drops.

If we are to take horses into unnatural situations involving manmade obstacles, and putting them under pressure to make snap decisions, we need to appreciate that they do not perceive the world as people do.

A horse cannot look at a change in height, however big, and make a snap decision on how high to jump or how much of an angle he must put into the descent to make a safe landing. This ability must be *learned* and can only happen when the horse is given time to gather this knowledge. When you give him time to feel his way, he can gain confidence to "have a go" and adjust on the way up or down to make a safe landing because he knows that you will leave him alone while he does. Interfering with a horse as he is making this judgment can seriously impede his ability to make the right decision.

The key is to start with one small step, maybe just a *threshold* (see *Over, Exercise 5,* p. 55) before building up to a flight of steps taken at speed. If you do not have steps available, try working with a podium—both from the ground and when riding.

In the photo below, you see a step with a small ditch on the landing side so Laura's horse must be comfortable to jump down before we even start trying to add a ditch.

On a cross-country course, steps, ditches, and drop fences are common.

Exercise 13 · Steps

A Approach a small step quietly and allow the horse to work out how he is going to negotiate it.

B Let the horse look.

C On a loose rein, so he can move his head freely, let him step down.

D As the steps get gradually higher, Laura leaves her horse to find his own way on a loose rein.

E She follows the same principles as above to give him courage to jump up.

F He jumps confidently up the steps because he's had time to work out how.

Side Story

Pearas and the Pole

Pearas is an all-round horse who does a bit of dressage and show jumping and we have used her in some of our photos because she has been such a success story for Carol, her owner. When I first met Pearas she was scared of a lot of things and showed it by going into instant flight, bucking and rearing to try to get away. Added to this, when she felt really under pressure, she kicked out and struck at her handler.

For over a year we helped Pearas rewrite her survival strategy and you will see through the photos in this book how well we have all worked together to bring her into the twenty-first century. But, as with all horses, she had something to teach us as we decided to take the photographs for the Jumping in Hand, *Over, Exercise 14.*

This is a horse that jumps well but sometimes completes the course too quickly, resulting in faults. When we walked her over the pole and asked her to stop immediately after it as requested in the exercise, she found it impossible to stop with the pole behind her. We began to see why Pearas needed to go fast when jumping: she did not like the pressure of the pole behind her.

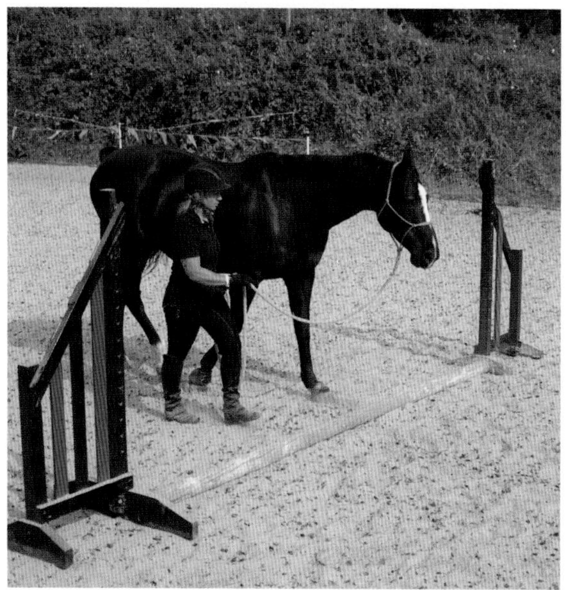

A Leading Pearas over the pole.

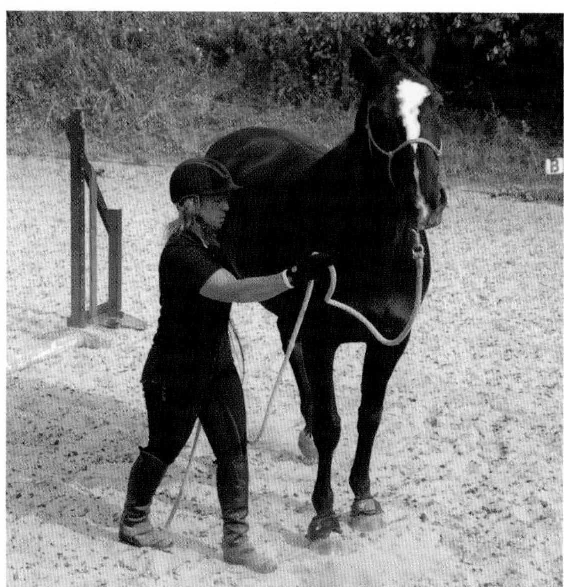

B Asking her to stop: see how her hind end has moved away from the pole?

To us humans, it seems ridiculous that a pole on the ground behind a horse should worry her, but to Pearas it was a real issue that was magnified when we increased the pace from walk to trot. The more pressure we put on her to stop after the pole, the more concerned she became so I made the following suggestion to Carol.

"Walk or trot her over the pole and quietly ask her to stop after it by just slowing your movement down. Do not force the issue, travel with her, continually asking her to stop and when she does, give her lots of praise." On the first attempt, Pearas stopped quietly about six strides from the pole. On the second attempt, it was three strides, on the third, Pearas stopped just after the pole without a problem.

Pearas is now jumping more accurately because she no longer runs away from the pressure of the pole behind her. By allowing her to choose her own stopping distance, she became comfortable that she was not going to be put under extra pressure when she was already on the edge of flight.

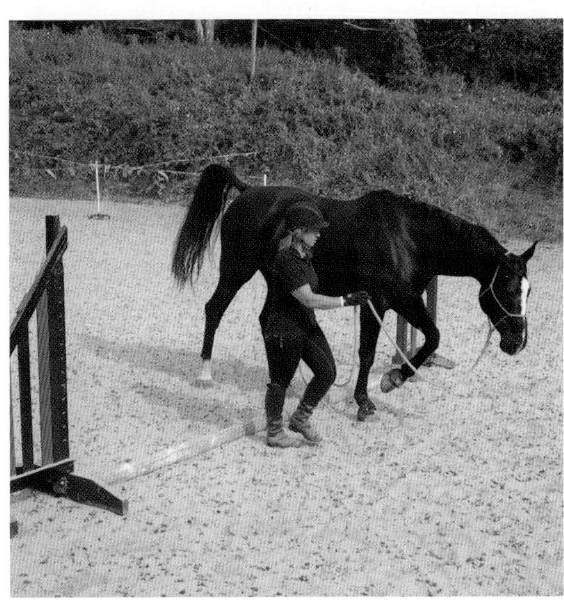

C On the next attempt, you can see she is tense by the shape of her tail.

D Carol is quietly asking her to stop, which she did just after this photograph.

14 JUMPING

Jumping safely in hand and under saddle.

It wasn't until I started Horse Agility with my horse that I realized I had never given her the opportunity to learn how to jump. I urge you to go out and try it yourself: running and jumping at various safe obstacles to see how much is involved in such a complex action. You need to gauge the distance as you approach, adjust your stride so that you take off in the right place, then decide how high to jump.

By starting with something as simple as a pole on the ground and raising it as your horse understands what is involved, you can begin to appreciate that horses need time to learn the skills of jumping. Horses are natural jumpers but on their terms—in nature. Everything changes with a rider on top and over jumps that are far more complex and brighter in color than those they would find out in their natural habitat.

By starting small and building to bigger obstacles your horse will become more careful and trust in your ability to place him at a jump while allowing to him find his own way. Once this is established you can begin to influence the footfall and he will respond to your request in the knowledge that you really do know what you are doing.

In the picture below, Carol releases her reins as she jumps without restricting her movement of the horse's head and neck.

Every horse, regardless of discipline, should be capable of clearing a small obstacle.

Exercise 14 · Jumping

A Jumping should not be exciting, it is like "dressage with jumps." Start by walking your horse calmly over a pole on the ground.

B Make sure the horse is comfortable crossing poles at walk and trot.

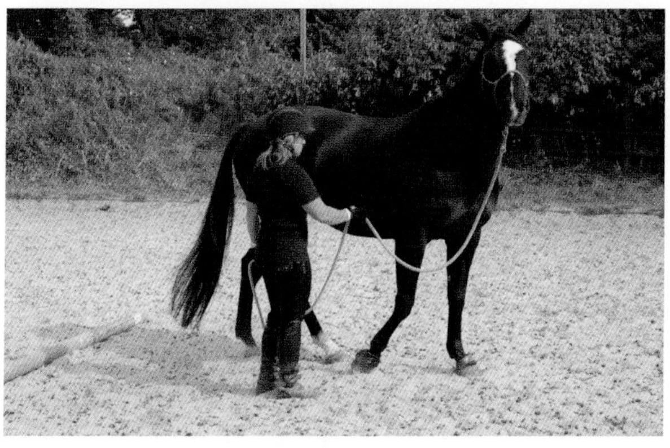

C After crossing the pole at walk, ask the horse to stop. You can see that this horse is not happy to stop with the pole behind her as she looks back at it (see "Pearas and the Pole," p. 80).

D The horse looks much happier in this picture.

E Now start to jump your horse in hand by traveling beside him at trot; you let him jump but go round the jump yourself. It is easier to do when there aren't any jump wings because you do not need to worry about the rope catching on the uprights.

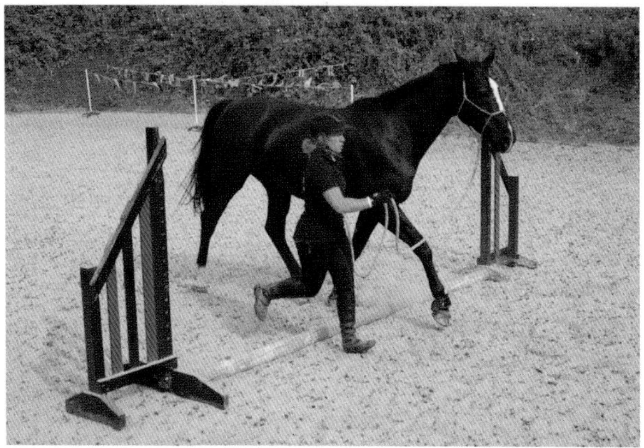

F Now introduce some jump wings because these can create a different pressure for the horse, and repeat the above stages.

G Never let the horse run on after the jump or take the jump in front of you as he may kick back after jumping.

H When you start riding, go right back to the beginning, walking over a pole first before you introduce the jump supports.

I Introduce low jumps, even if the horse doesn't quite jump at first.

J Build up to higher jumps. If you or the horse lose confidence just go back a stage until you both feel comfortable again.

15 WATER

From walking in water to jumping it at speed.

There is always a bigger crowd at the water jump in any cross-country competition than at any other obstacle. This is for lots of reasons but mainly it's the splendid sight of a horse jumping into water, and the rider getting a good soaking if she falls off! But, let's not entertain the crowd other than with good horsemanship; let's prepare your horse to jump bravely into water and out of it. Water and horses should be a fun combination.

Water and horses can be a fun combination!

Exercise 15 · Water

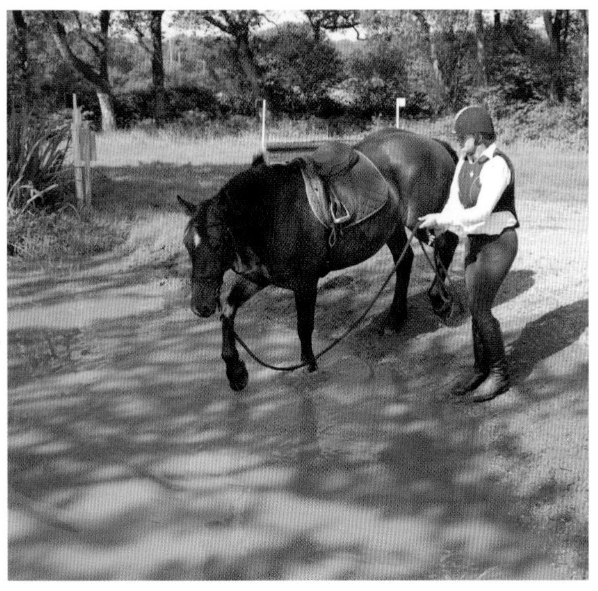

A Start on the ground by allowing the horse to enter and explore the water: let him splash and explore this new "toy."

B If he just wants to stand in the water let him do it.

C With the preparation carried out on the ground, it is much easier for the horse to go into the water when you are riding.

D When walking into the water is established you can start to trot.

E Let him find the water a fun place but be prepared to get wet!

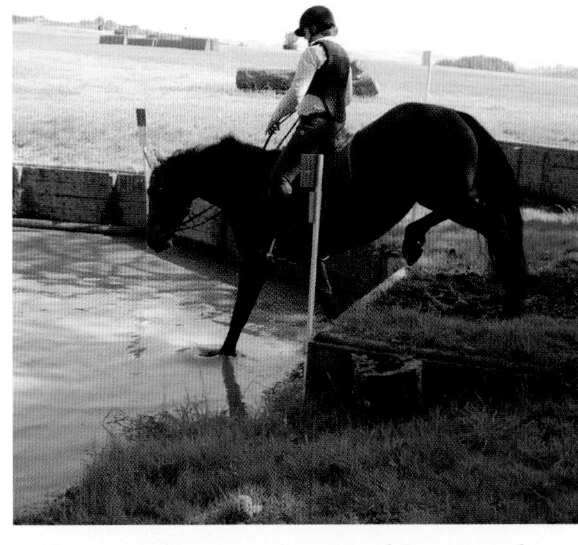

F Place a small jump at the edge of the water of a type that the horse has confidently jumped before; all you are doing now is putting the two things together.

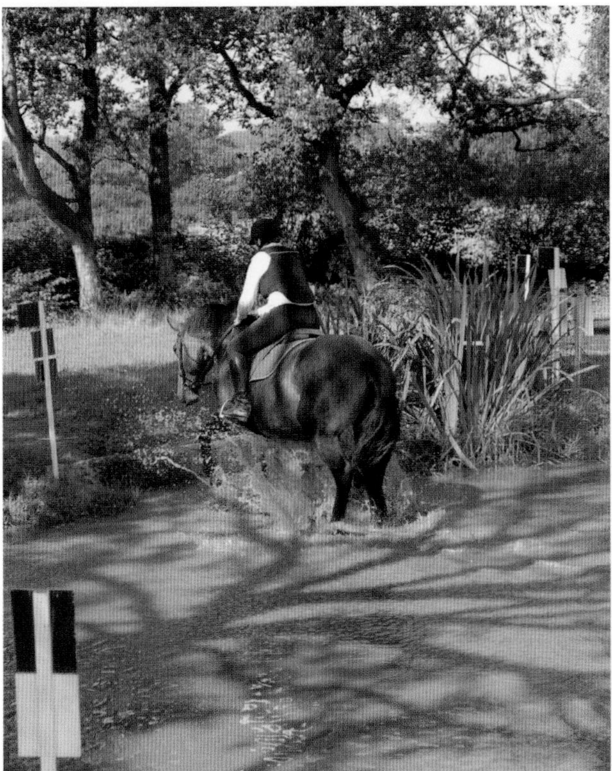

G Having jumped in, it's time to jump out.

H This horse is confidently trotting through water focusing on the jump out. He knows how to move through water and, as he gains in experience and confidence, we can start looking for greater water challenges.

16 BEACHES

Riding on the sand and in the surf.

Galloping into the crashing breakers on a white sandy beach must be one of the most dreamed-about horse-riding experiences. I was lucky enough to live for many years a few hundred yards from the three-mile-long beach at Woolacombe in Devon, England, and the flat white sands became my arena. I learned a lot about how horses perceive the rolling white surf and spent many hours playing on the ground and in the saddle as I accustomed them to the sights and sounds of the seaside. The beach in these photographs is farther down the coast with lots to keep us busy as you can see from the pictures.

There's nothing like galloping down a deserted stretch of beach!

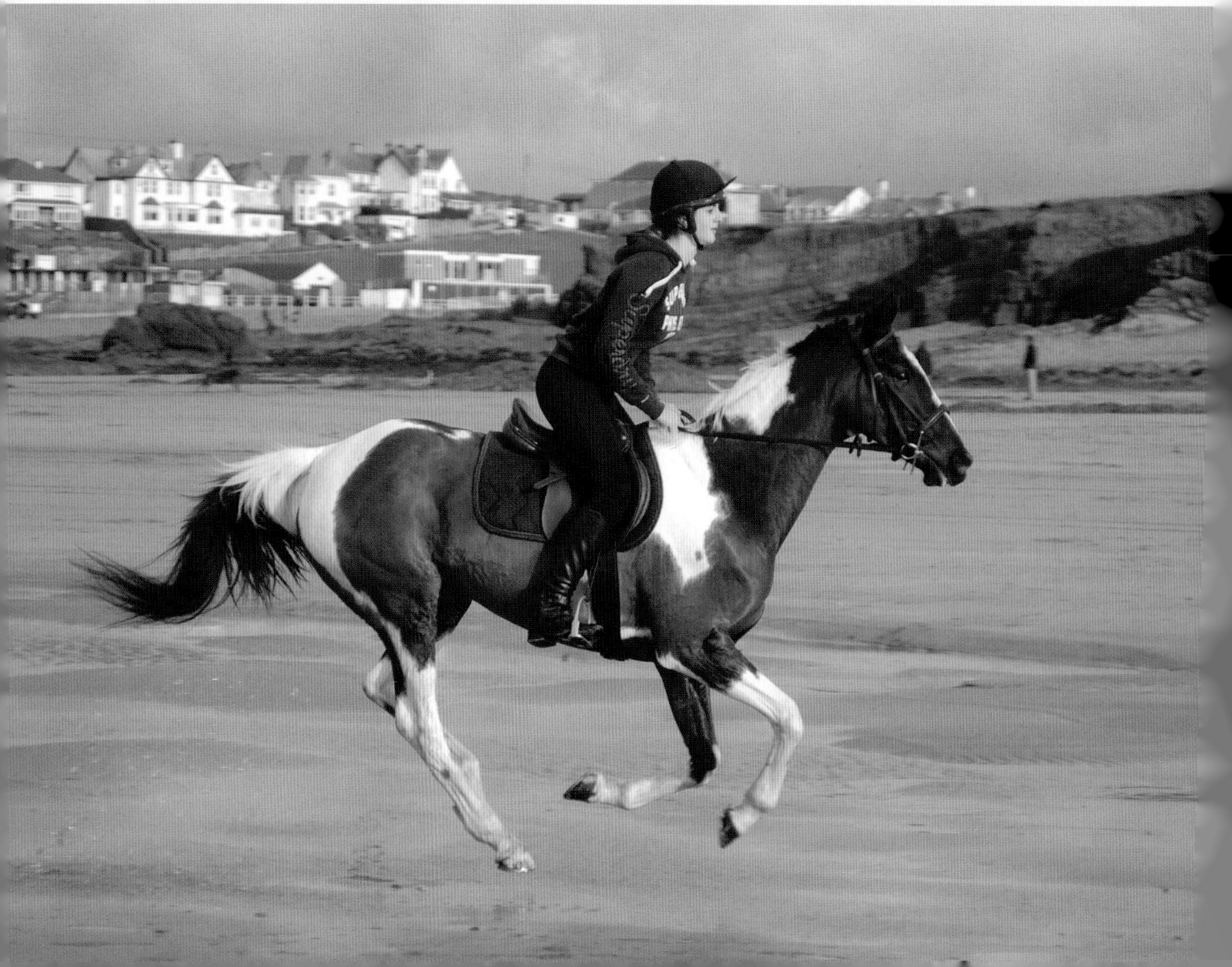

Exercise 16 · Beaches

A You may want to work on the ground first to let your horse get his feet wet—and yours, too.

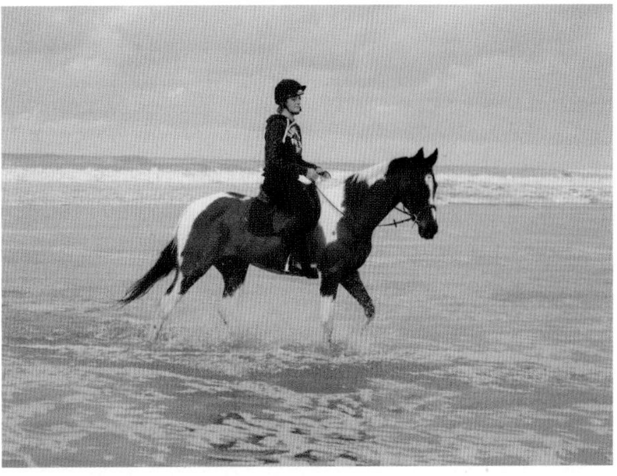

B Paddle about in the shallow water first once you are on board so that your horse can feel the water moving back and forth around his legs.

C The small white waves might look like solid poles rolling towards your horse's legs so if he seems afraid, give him time to understand that they are not hard.

D Allow him to stand in the water and let the waves roll in.

E Then off you go!

F At the end of the fun, horse and rider relax and head home.

"Sound Advice"

Believe in Your Horse.

It goes without saying that the more time you spend in the company of your horse, the better you will know each other. If his behavior suddenly changes, in even the smallest way, you are more likely to notice it and try to find out why. It's like that gut feeling that something "isn't quite right."

For instance, supposing your horse usually grazes with his friends but one day you see that he is away down the pasture on his own. It may be that he has found a tasty patch of grass and the others have wandered off without him noticing, or perhaps he's been injured and unable to travel with the rest of the herd. It could be worth just going down there and checking him over.

Whenever your horse does something out of character, consider why: he might be trying to tell you something as the following story recounts.

We have a large area of wild country in the west of England called Bodmin Moor. Hundreds of years ago, it was extensively mined for tin and is peppered with old mineshafts, ruined buildings, and industrial archaeology. It is a horse rider's paradise because there is a lot of wide open space to gallop and play.

One summer's day a group of friends set out for a day ride and among them was Jenny, riding her young horse Jazz. The horse had been with her since he was a foal and she had trained and started him herself so they knew each other very well. As the friends traveled over the open moorland Jazz suddenly stopped and refused to go forward. He had never done this before and as Jenny tried to get him to move, he became very difficult, spinning round and giving little half rears. Jenny's friends encouraged her to push him on and show him who was in charge. Despite her confusion at Jazz's unusual behavior the advice from her friends seemed sensible; she had heard young horses did test their riders sometimes. She drove him forward and to everyone's horror the ground collapsed beneath them as an abandoned mineshaft opened up beneath Jazz's feet. As he fell Jenny managed to throw herself to safety and was uninjured but it took the fire brigade many hours to rescue poor Jazz. Jenny says that her gut instinct told her that Jazz must be telling her something, but she didn't listen.

Jazz survived his ordeal but never entirely trusted Jenny again.

A Braced, ready to run away. **B** Ready to run through. **C** Gaining courage as she prepares to run under. **D** Coming through but dropping her head to avoid the branches.

PART TWO: **UNDER**

It was my horse Secret who taught me about going under things. As I said at the start of this book, every horse has a weak area and Secret's is going underneath. So this section is dedicated to her with grateful thanks for showing me how to help her overcome this very natural fear.

Think of horses in the wild. When do they ever need to go under anything by choice? Horses are animals of the wide open plains; they do graze in the woods and under low branches but it is always with one eye on the exit if they need to run. In hot open country they have been seen in caves avoiding the searing sun and drinking from pools that have collected in them, but this is an exception.

We expect our domestic horse to go under things on numerous occasions. Into buildings, trailers, under archways—the list is pretty long. By being aware of this fear in your horse and setting up each obstacle sensitively, you can help him come to terms with the pressure over his head.

In this simple sequence you can see Secret telling me how difficult she finds it going under this obstacle. Putting more pressure on her will only make it worse so I make it easy at the start, slowly building the challenge as she learns that there is nothing to fear.

1 TUNNELS

Passing under archways and tunnels.

When you have a horse that doesn't like going under things, you notice how many places he needs to do this: even quite high road tunnels with the roof some distance above the horse's head can cause him to shrink down a little as he passes underneath. By starting with very simple tunnels as little as just one pole you can help your horse understand that the "roof" isn't going to fall and bang his head.

As he becomes more confident you can drape flags or decorations above the entrance so that he feels them brush his ears—without hurting him.

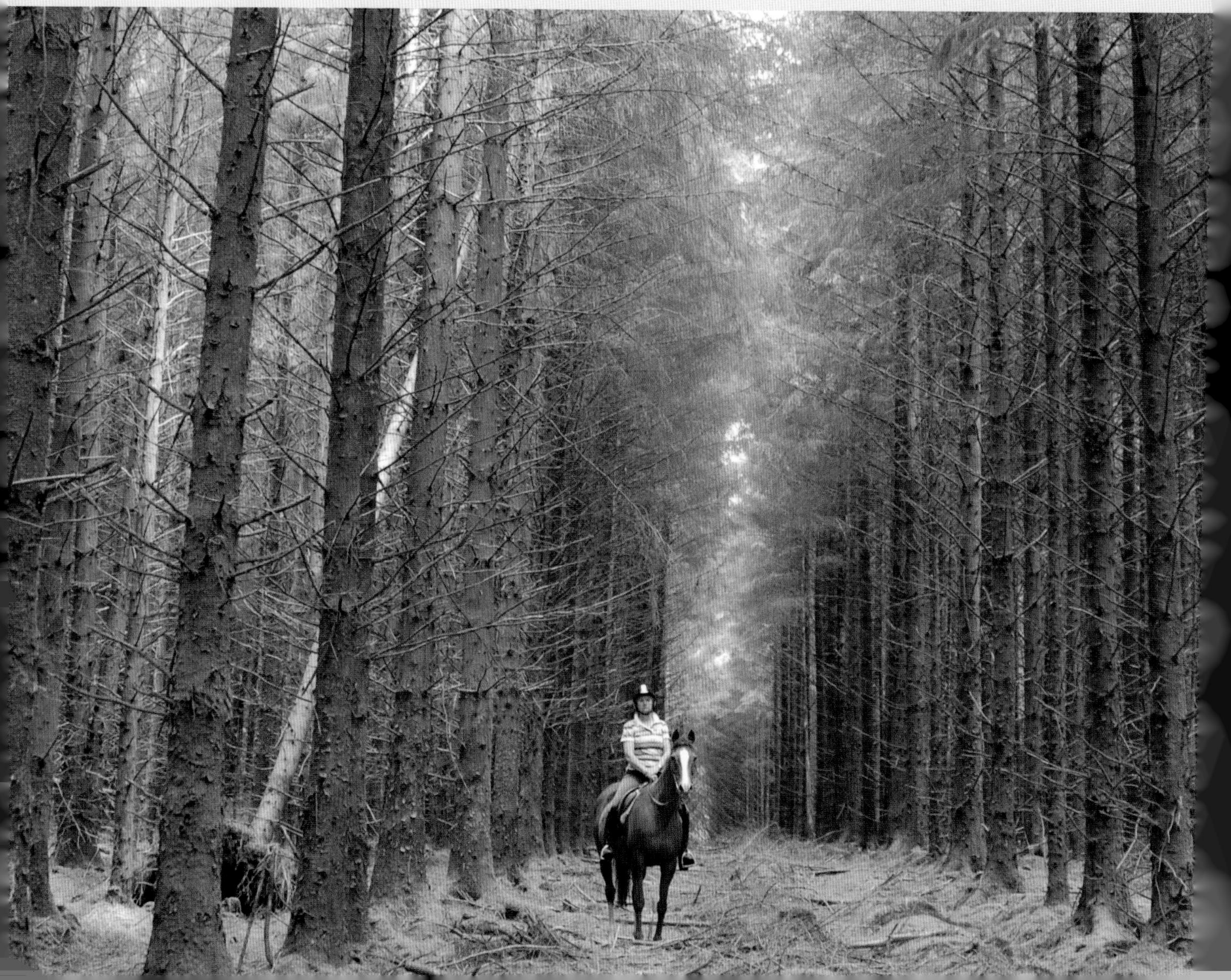

The trees in our woodland form a natural, high-roofed tunnel.

Exercise 1 · Tunnels

A Start with a simple frame: this is an old tent frame.

B Add thickness to the frame with material. This is wind-breaking netting that you might see in a garden. It is light and much less likely to blow away.

C Slowly extend the cover over the frame.

D Now you are going to ride through but make sure you can lean right down on your horse's neck before you do.

E With only half the frame covered, ride underneath.

F Now cover the whole frame and ride through.

Side Story

What on Earth Is the Use of a Curtain or Carwash?

When I traveled in North America a few years ago I stayed with a lovely family in Denver, Colorado, who had a whole herd of miniature ponies. The family liked their ponies to have free access to outside winter and summer, but also wanted them to have an area that stayed pretty well above freezing in winter so they didn't get too cold. The bodies of all these little ponies in the barn generated enough heat to keep the air above freezing, but with the door wide open it was soon lost, especially at night when the ponies were mainly just standing indoors.

The family took the idea from the cold-storage industry where thick plastic strips are used to keep the cold in the storage areas while frozen foods are carried in and out of the open door. They hung heavy plastic strips across the doorway so the ponies could travel in and out without too much heat being lost. Ventilation in the roof meant there was always a good supply of fresh air, too.

"But how did you teach them they could push through?" I asked.

"We didn't," replied Kirsty. "They wanted to go in and out so they just worked out that by pushing on the flaps, they could."

It just shows that horses will quickly work things out when the need is there, in this case basic food and shelter. It made me wonder what other skills they could learn if we just gave them the tools and the motivation to find out how they work.

I have since found using these thick plastic curtains to keep horses warm in winter is relatively common. This young pony lives in the mountains of Austria and very quickly learned how to negotiate the unusual obstacle.

2 CURTAINS

Passing under curtains and car washes.

This seemingly simple obstacle poses a real challenge for a lot of horses. If you start very simply, and slowly build the pressure, they gain the courage to pass through before too long. The curtain has many elements to consider: the horse has to go under and through as well as having to "push" what looks like a solid wall of ribbons. So assume nothing because if you over face your horse early on, it can take longer to regain his confidence than just making it easy from the start.

Through the curtain, without hesitation!

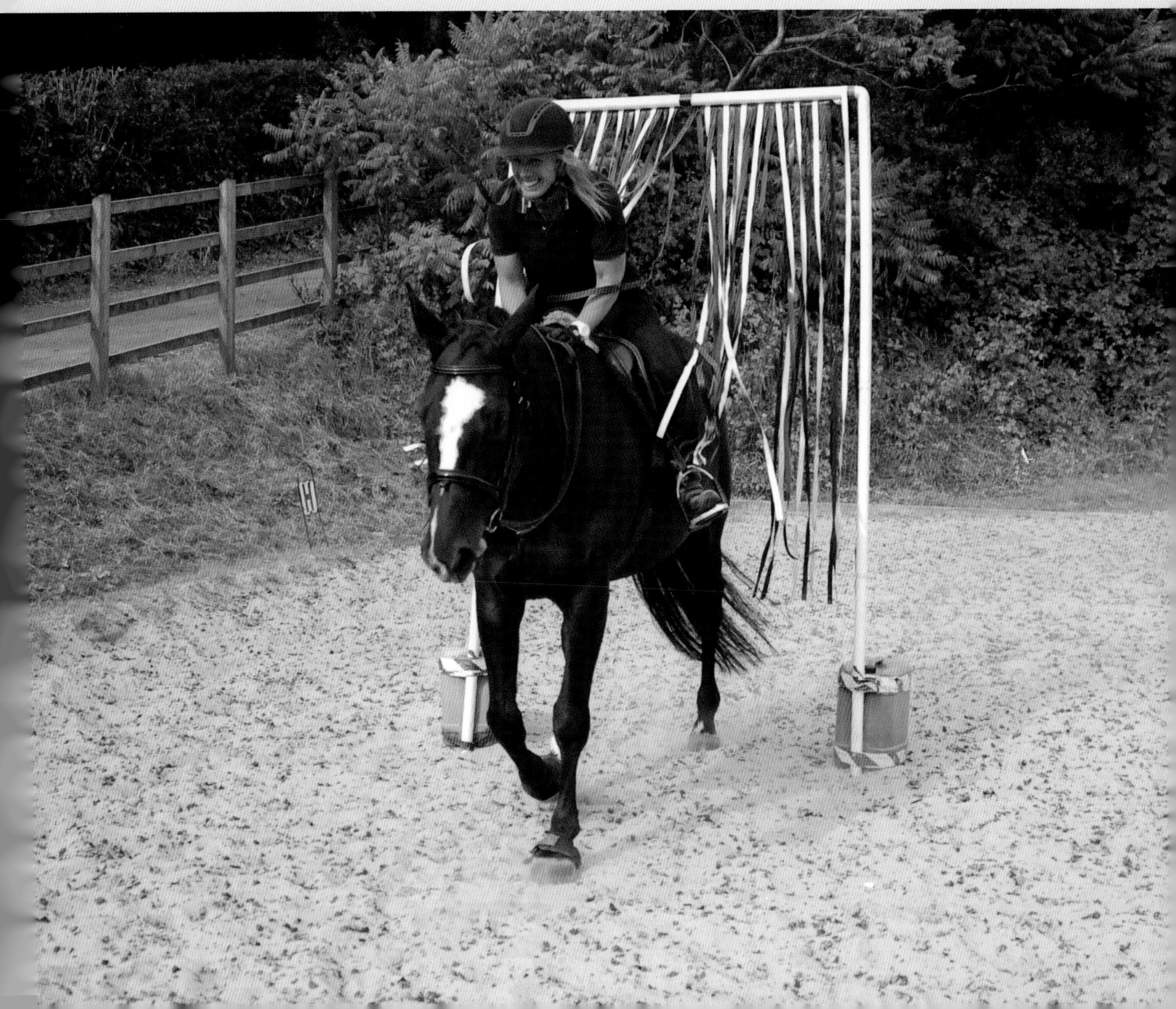

Exercise 2 · Curtains

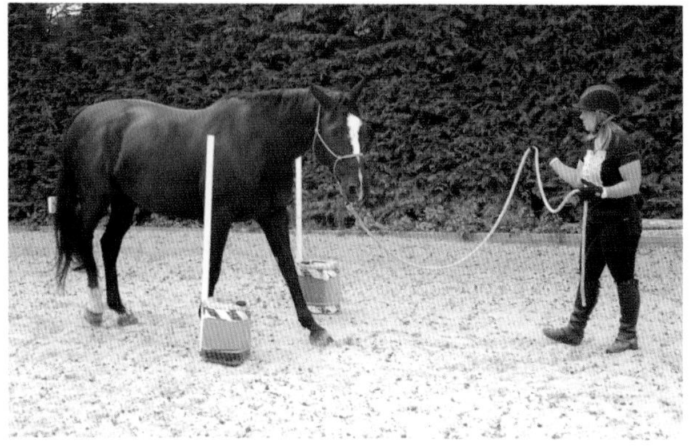

A Start by making sure your horse can pass through a narrow gap.

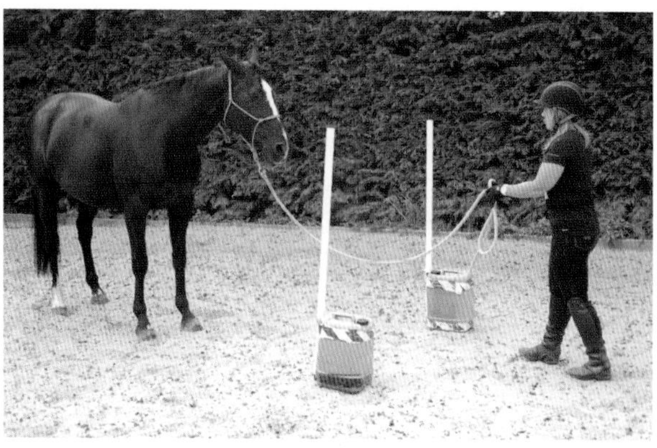

B Ask the horse to wait, walk through yourself, and stand well out of the way.

C When you are ready, invite the horse to join you.

D Add ribbons to the top of the frame, but tie them back as shown.

E Ask the horse to wait, and, after walking through yourself and standing out of the way, ask the horse to join you.

F Now drop just one ribbon and ask again; it is amazing what a difference one single ribbon can make.

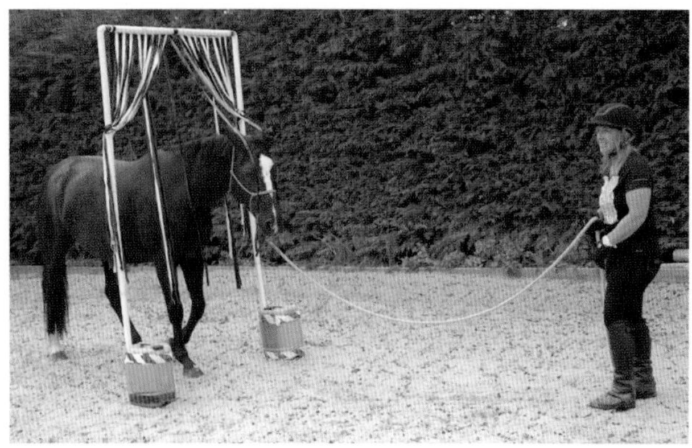

G Drop a few more ribbons down, but not too many.

H Keep adding ribbons until your horse can walk through the whole curtain without a trace of worry.

I Now you are ready to ride. You may wish to start by riding through the uprights before adding the curtain. I have started with the curtain tied back here. Make sure you can lean right down on your horse's neck first.

J Then drop one ribbon.

K Now drop two ribbons and so on, until you can ride straight through.

L Here, Carol decides that carrying part of the curtain would make an interesting challenge while riding.

3 BRANCHES

Passing under low tree branches.

We have a horse sport in Europe called *Le Trec*. It is a three-part competition with an orienteering phase, a control of paces in walk and canter, and a ridden obstacle course. One of the obstacles is riding under low branches and the branches are measured to be about 9 inches (20cm) above each horse's withers. That's not very high and because the competition is timed, a lot of people are doing this at the canter. I think that's pretty impressive.

You never know what you might meet out on the trail, and preparing for overhead obstacles puts you a step ahead.

Make sure you can lean right down onto your horse's neck before you start riding under low branches or your horse may continue on his own as you dangle from the trees behind him on the trail.

Exercise 3 · Branches

A Create a simple frame—we have used push-together plumbing pipe here—and ensure the horse can walk under it.

B Add a few natural leaves, branches, or plants.

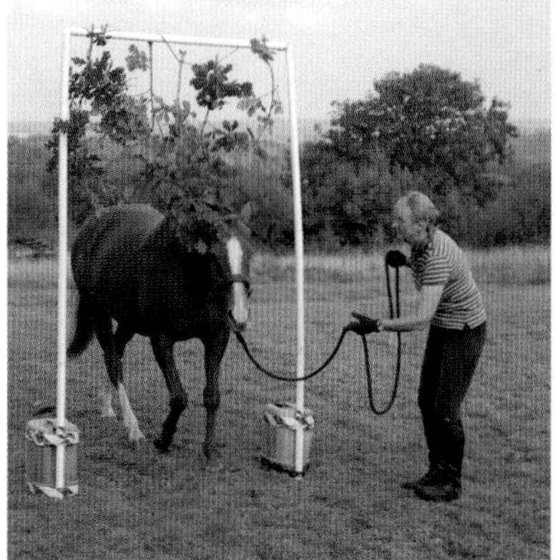

C Slowly add to the leaves and branches, but don't go too quickly here.

D Make sure you can lean right down on the horse's back before riding under the branches or you may pull the whole structure over.

E First, ride under one branch then add more as your horse relaxes.

F Here's a lovely, natural obstacle of low trees over a track in the woods.

Side Story

The Flag and the Olympic Torch

In 2012 Great Britain hosted the Olympic Games and although a great success, the famous British weather made its presence felt with one of the wettest summers on record. A few weeks before the Games I was asked to teach Horse Agility in the county of Dorset. The day dawned with gale-force winds and rain coming down in sheets. I fully expected the group of eight to cancel but six hardy souls turned up—the other two having been trapped by rising flood water and unable to leave home.

Despite the appalling weather we had a really fun day with the "scary corner" of festive decorations, flags, and streamers looking at its best: flags standing straight out and fairly roaring in the wind. Initially, every horse was pretty scared by the flags but as the day wore on, they soon began to realize that bits of printed fabric attached to poles and blowing in the wind did not hurt. Eventually everyone stood together on the corner just because they thought it was a fun thing to do.

The next week two of the girls were asked if they could follow the Olympic Torch on horseback as it was carried through a village near their stables. Of course, the girls were delighted to be invited to take part in such an historic event. As they followed the Torch, a member of the crowd rushed out brandishing a large Union Jack flag on a short pole and thrust it into one of the girl's hands. It could have been a disaster making international front page news as a terrified horse complete with rider carrying the Union flag galloped past the Torch. But the Horse Agility training saved the day and the horse simply looked back at the flag and seemed to say, "Yes, I know what that is and I'm okay with it."

4 FLAGS

Helping the horse accept flags above him and carrying them.

Even if you never intend to ride in a grand parade, carrying a flag is a fun skill to work through. If you can ride with a flag then any flags at shows and beside the road will never worry your horse.

Carol and her horse calmly carry the flag for England.

Exercise 4 · Flags

A Start by helping the horse to accept a flag while it is rolled or tied up.

B Gradually unfurl the flag and let the horse explore how it moves and feels.

C If he is unhappy you may need to show the flag to the horse briefly then remove it before he becomes afraid. This is called *Advance and Retreat* and is outlined in *Blueprint 3* (p. 11).

D Here the flag is held away from the horse.

E Continue moving the flag towards and away from the horse until he accepts it on his body.

F Remember the flag must be seen from everywhere, even right over his head.

G Now try moving the horse—not the flag—and *Advance and Retreat* towards it.

H Keep working on this until the horse is relaxed and happy about it.

I You can use flags to create interest in your work: here we have created a flag weave.

J When the horse is comfortable with the flag while you are on the ground, you can now ride and ask a friend to use the same techniques as above to help the horse accept the flag.

K Or you can ride to and from a flag that is on the ground.

L Do not be tempted to pick the flag up too soon, but if you do get it wrong, remember to drop the flag if the horse becomes very frightened.

5 UMBRELLAS

Staying calm around umbrellas.

When I first started using umbrellas to help horses become braver, a skeptical onlooker asked why on earth I would need to get them used to an umbrella. After my simple explanation that anything novel to a horse is worth using as a tool to gain their trust, I could see she was not convinced.

However, it's amazing how the ether works in mysterious ways. The following week this same skeptic was riding outside in a dressage competition. Half-way through her test it started to rain and immediately the spectators began to put up umbrellas. Needless to say, the horse took one look at this growing forest of brightly colored "mushrooms" and left the arena. I'm glad to say my skeptical onlooker was game enough to admit her lack of imagination and regularly attends training days with her horse who no longer spooks at umbrellas, push chairs (strollers), dogs, trash bags, flags…well you get the picture!

While you may never want to ride with an umbrella, it's fun to know you can! You never know what you might meet out on the trail.

You may never want to ride with an umbrella…but it's fun to know you can!

Exercise 5 · Umbrellas

A Use a safe umbrella with no spikes; children's are the best. Show the closed umbrella to your horse.

B Undo the clasp so that it looks less like a stick.

C Rub the unfurled, but not completely open, umbrella on the horse's body and use *Advance and Retreat* as outlined in *Blueprint 3* (p. 11). Accustom the horse to it.

D Open the umbrella right up and move it around the horse. Be very careful not to poke him.

E Repeat all the above stages when riding. Always remember you can drop the umbrella at any time.

F Don't open the umbrella too quickly.

RIBBONS

Wearing rosettes, ribbons, and sashes safely.

It's a wonderful sight to see people who have done well in a competition go galloping around the arena decked in ribbons and sashes presented to them and tied to various parts of the horse's bridle. But it's worth practicing this at home first.

Performing the triumphant champion's gallop, hand raised in recognition of the crowd's support is one thing, but to have a horse bolting in terror as ribbons flap about his face and chest is quite another. So let's assume that one day that "champion" will be you and your horse and prepare in advance for the great day.

Perhaps better placement of our ribbons, next time!

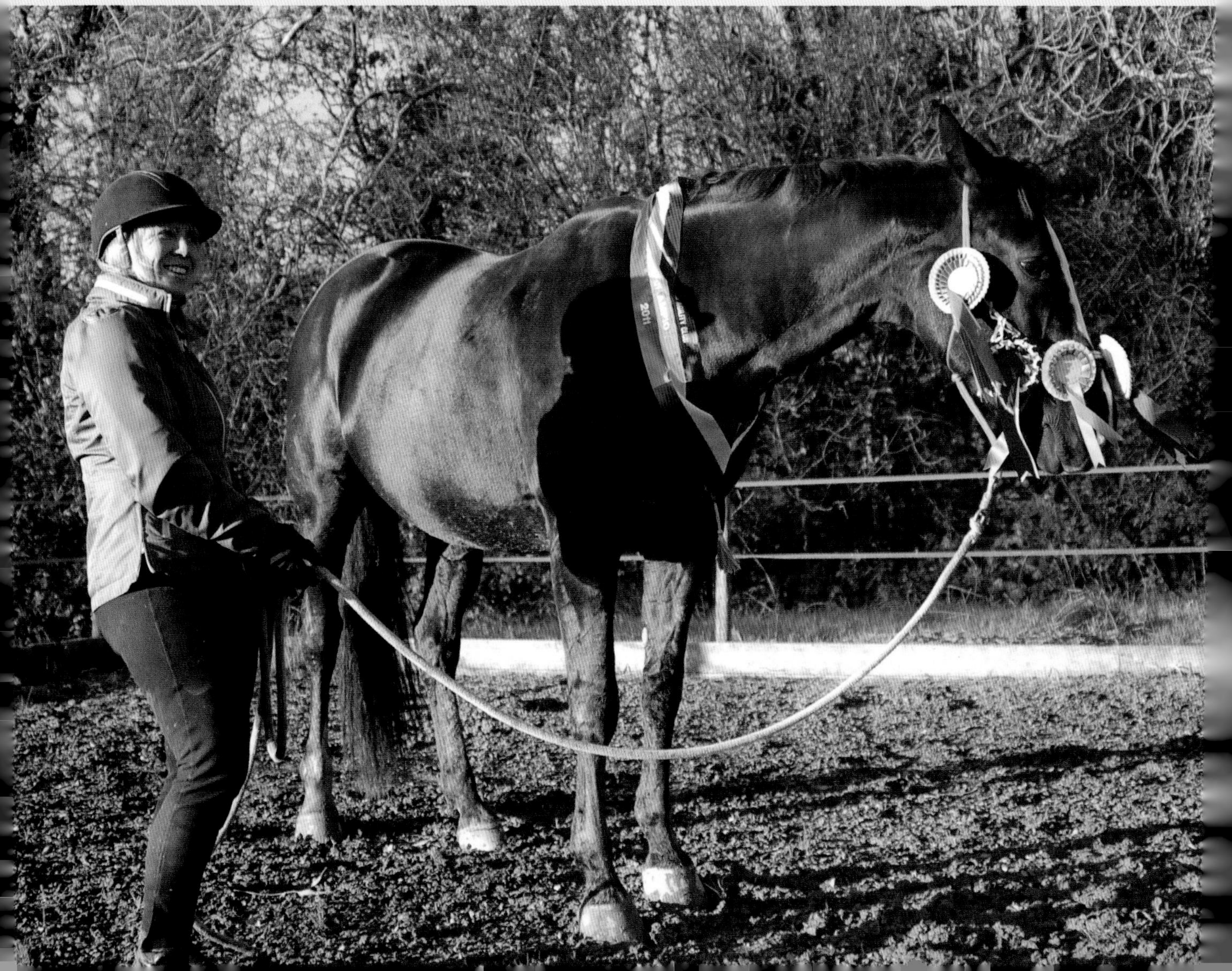

Exercise 6 · Ribbons

A Use a flag to get your horse used to things flapping around his face and neck.

B Use *Advance and Retreat: Blueprint 3* (p. 11), to help the horse accept one ribbon.

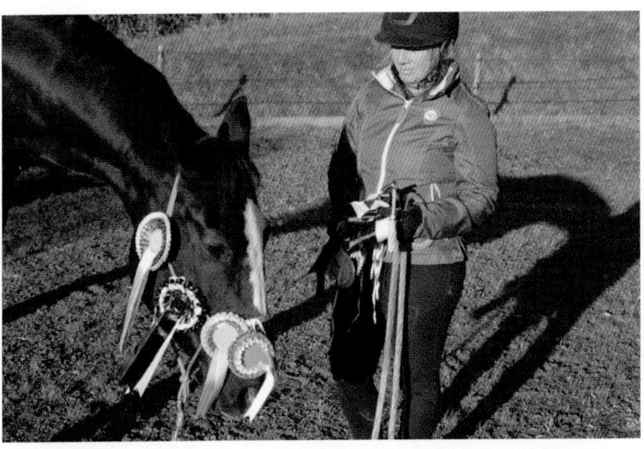

C Add ribbons one by one as the horse accepts them.

D Let the horse see the sash and feel it on his body before putting it round his neck.

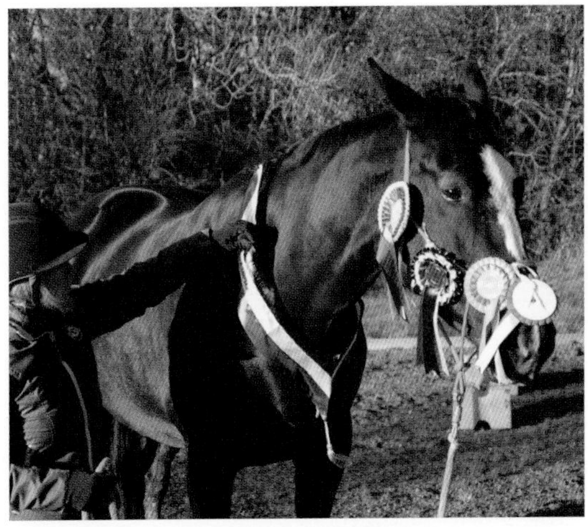

E When you do put the sash round the neck, use *Advance and Retreat* to help the horse.

F Let the horse move with ribbons because they may rub him and make a noise as they flutter against his face and he needs to get used to that.

7 FLY SPRAY

Accepting the sound, feel and smell of spray bottles.

Sometimes you feel you just have to use fly spray. It's ridiculously expensive and only seems to keep the flies away for a few minutes, but it makes us feel that we've at least done something to help our horse cope with the misery of flies.

Natural horses cope well because they stand close together and use each other's swishing tails to keep the insects at bay. But if you want to ride, they don't have that option. Getting the insecticide onto the horse can be just as stressful—more so for the horse—than the irritating flies so it's worth helping them get used to the application before the flies get started in the warmer weather. Whenever I use spray I don't just march up to my horse and shock her with a cold, noisy spurt of it, I spend time showing her what I intend to do so she is prepared.

I never tie my horses; if my horse is not ready to accept the spray, she has the choice to leave.

Your horse should be willing to stand quietly, without being restrained, while you apply spray products.

Exercise 7 • Fly Spray

A Fill an old fly spray bottle with water and, by using *Advance and Retreat—Blueprint 3* (p. 11), help your horse get used to the noise first.

B Let him smell the flyspray. It may have a pleasant fragrance to you but a horse may have quite a different idea about it.

C When you start to spray, the horse may be scared so you need to keep going until you feel him relax, then stop spraying.

D If you stop while he is afraid, you will help him think that by going into flight mode he stopped the noise and that's the complete opposite of what you want him to think. This is the principle of *Advance and Retreat.*

E Here the horse has relaxed so I have stopped spraying.

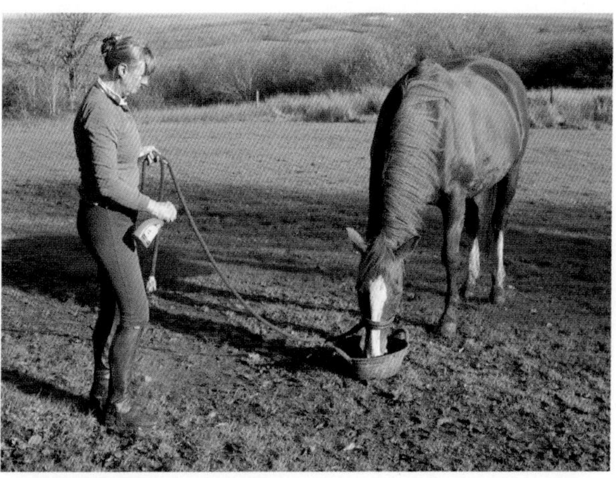

F Sometimes making the spraying sound when the horse is eating can create a pleasant association with the noise.

8 SADDLES

Introducing saddles and dealing with saddling issues.

To me, putting a saddle on a horse is something that must be done by mutual agreement. I never tie my horse to put a saddle on because when he leaves as I approach with it, he is telling me something. The main reason horses do not like their saddle is because it hurts—or did hurt once—and they remember. Using a saddle that causes pain must be dealt with immediately as even a short ride with an ill-fitting saddle can cause irreparable damage.

Helping the horse erase the memory of pain can take slightly longer but it is possible. A gelding that lived with us for a while would always turn to bite me as I placed the saddle on his back. There was no pain but he remembered that once there was. Instead of telling him off, I used to stroke his face as he turned to bite so that putting the saddle on became a pleasant operation for him.

Saddling should be a calm, agreeable experience for all concerned.

Saddling should be a calm, pleasant experience for all concerned.

Exercise 8 · Saddles

A Sometimes I just take the saddle into the pasture and place it on my horse's back without making any other demands of her.

B I expect my horse to engage with me as I approach. When she does not, I know I need to think carefully about the saddle and how I am riding her.

C When I approach, I speak to her and give her a rub.

D When I put the saddle on, I lift it high and place it lightly onto her back.

E Then I rub her again.

F If she feels like it she can carry it home for me.

9 OWL HOLE

Going under the rim of agility hoops and cross-country jumps with overhead components.

An Owl Hole cross-country jump is an example of an obstacle that is over, under and through. Most riders see it as just under as their horse jumps over and through many different obstacles on a course, but the Owl Hole is a bit of a one-off in that it's all three.

A simple obstacle that can help your horse learn to combine all three elements of over, under, through is the Horse Agility hoop. It has been specifically designed so that it can be taken to pieces slowly thus building the challenge of jumping through a hoop. The Owl Hole is just a very elaborate and rather more solid hoop, so if you start simply, and build the skills in small stages, you can prepare the horse at home without having to build an elaborate cross-country obstacle.

We build our hoops out of land-drainage pipe, which is light. There is a long piece of pipe that forms the main overhead arch, and a shorter piece of pipe that clips to it to form the lower part of the hoop.

The "Owl Hole" cross-country jump is an impressive obstacle! If you can jump under this, what can't you do?

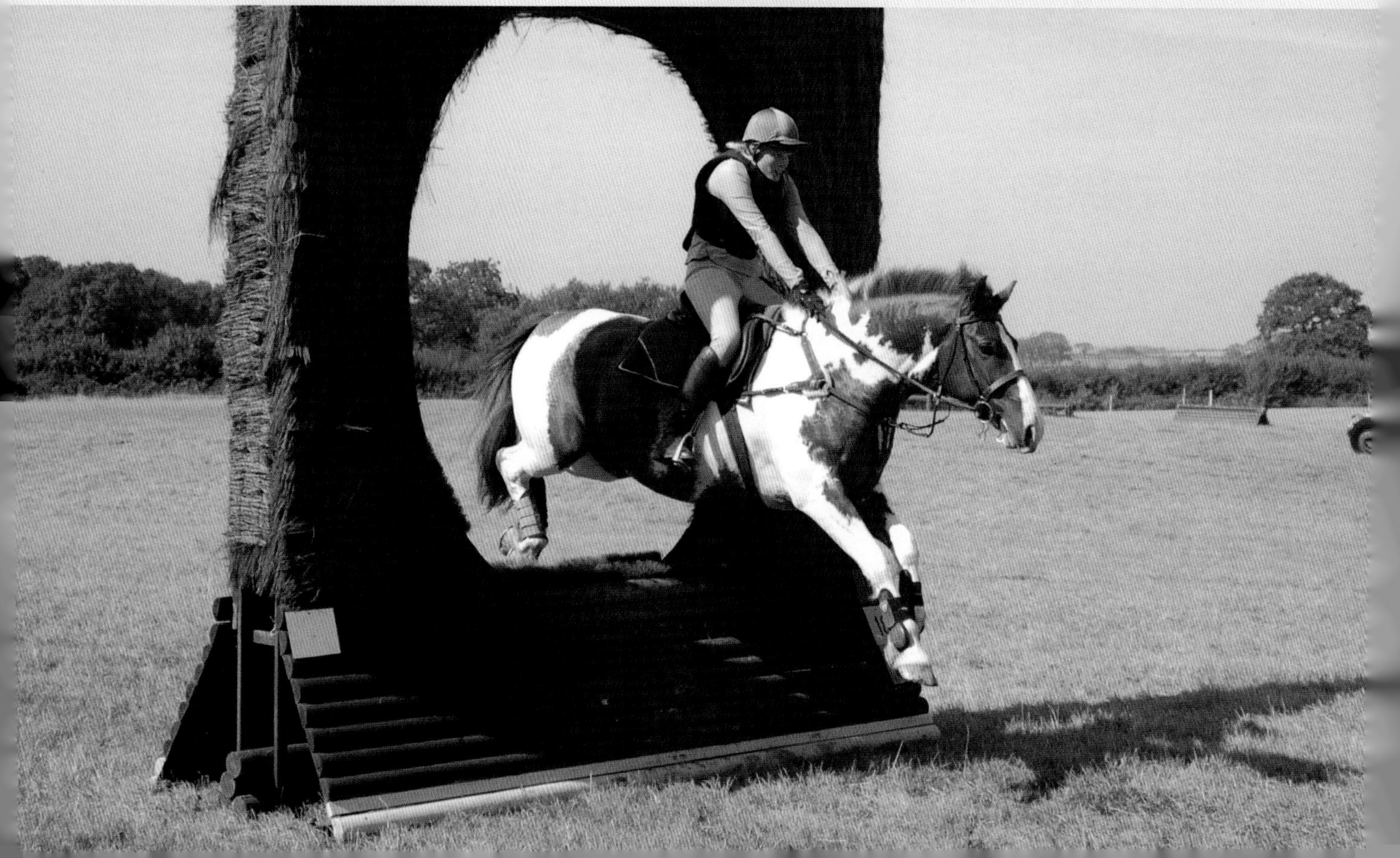

Exercise 9 · Owl Hole

A Start with a plain arch and let the horse become used to passing under and through.

B Introduce the lower part of the hoop; you may want to start with it right down on the ground at first, then raise it as your horse becomes comfortable.

C As the horse begins to understand that he is to go through the hoop you can begin to pass the lead rope hand to hand round the upright part of the main arch so that you are not jumping in front of the horse.

D Begin to increase the pace.

E Increase the height of the lower part of the hoop until the horse is actually jumping.

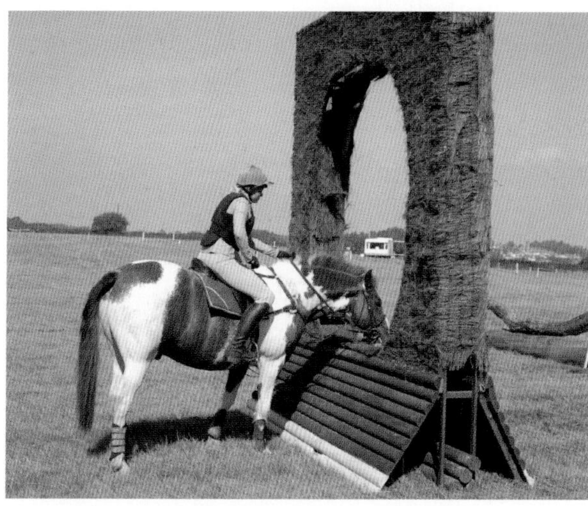

F Even though you may have practiced this as home, and perhaps even built a hoop big enough to jump through, it's worth letting the horse inspect the real obstacle before you jump through it.

"Sound Advice"

From Relaxed to Racing in a Tenth of a Second

Where do you go to "escape?" Your bed? A nice warm bath? Or walking in beautiful countryside? Where do you feel as though your batteries are being recharged?

To remain mentally well everyone needs a place to just stop, wind down, and let his or her brain have some quiet time. In the twenty-first century we're not awfully good at this; some of us actually have to schedule this time into our calendar to ever let it happen.

I believe every living creature needs this quiet time and, of course, that includes our horses.

Where is your horse's "escape?" His stall? Or is he constantly bothered by a threatening neighbor or a noisy environment? His pasture? Or do the flies drive him to distraction? It's really worth thinking about the down time your horse needs if he is to remain emotionally well.

All this comfortable living has its downside: we don't actually learn anything in our "comfort zone," we have to step out of that cozy place into what's called the "learning zone." But this discomfort doesn't need to be painful, just a little feeling of wanting to solve the problem that's causing the discomfort so we can get back into the place we're comfortable again.

That's all any of us are trying to do: solve problems to make life more comfortable, including horses. Unfortunately we often aren't too good at reading the body language of a horse that is trying to solve a problem and we go on piling on the pressure while he's trying to think.

Bothering a horse when he is in this thinking state is like someone asking you questions while you're on the phone trying to sort out an unpaid electric bill. You're under pressure already because you have the anxiety of losing your electricity and someone else is demanding even more from you. Eventually you will snap. This is where you have moved into the "flight" zone: you do and say things often out of character. All you want to do is sort the problem at hand and make life comfortable again. Once you're in the flight zone you aren't thinking, you just want to run away to a place where there is no pressure.

If we put this in a horse context, let's say someone is riding along the road; her horse is relaxed and easy until suddenly he spots a plastic bag caught in the bushes. He stops and tries to work out what it is. What happens if, without a moment's hesitation, the rider starts kicking and pushing, piling more pressure on the horse to get past that bag? He'll go into the flight mode because he feels under threat and just wants to get somewhere safe, and that's probably home. When he's able to move his feet that's where he'll go but if he's held by the rider he may buck, rear, or spin to try and get back to where he feels safe.

If you get to know what your horse looks like when he is thinking and trying to work out whether he should run or stay, that is the moment to just leave him alone and give him space to learn about the new object so that next time he'll remember that it was safe.

A As we approach the gate Ricky is happy with me being on his left side. **B** Now his body language has changed. Not only am I in front of him but he has an obstacle to negotiate. There's a lot to think about. **C** I ask Ricky to come through the gap. **D** He's already bent away from me because I'm now on his right side. With the added pressure of the gap all he wants to do is get away.

PART THREE: THROUGH

To humans, when we talk about traveling through something, we usually mean a path with obstacles on both sides, but I believe it isn't quite the same for a horse. Because of the way a horse views the world, when he sees something on one side, his other side isn't aware of its existence because of the way in which the eye-to-brain connections are made up. So a horse may look as though he is hurrying between two pressure points but in reality only one side is causing the problem. Well, this is my theory anyway.

Have you ever spent ages getting your horse past a scary object only to have to repeat the whole procedure when you turn around and go past it from the opposite direction? That's because on the way out only half his brain saw the scary thing; now on the return journey, the other half of the brain has to learn about it too.

When you travel through a narrow place with your horse I believe it is only one side that's frightened. Because he is unable to flee due to the other side of him being blocked by a wall or fence—or a hu-

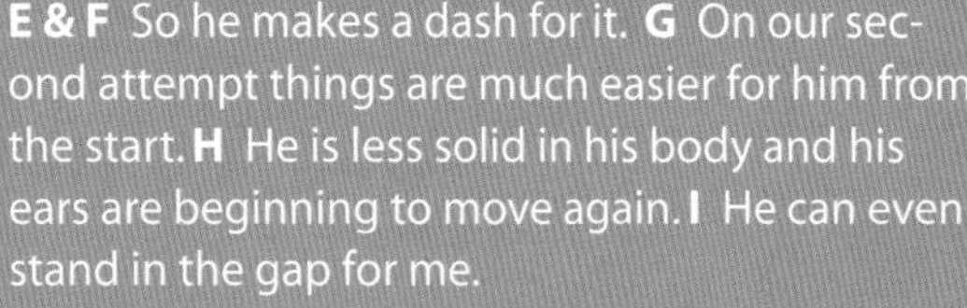

E & F So he makes a dash for it. **G** On our second attempt things are much easier for him from the start. **H** He is less solid in his body and his ears are beginning to move again. **I** He can even stand in the gap for me.

man, he goes into flight mode and rushes forward. The feeling of being trapped is a very natural condition for a horse, and one you can help him override to some extent as he rewrites his three-million-year-old risk assessment.

You cannot change how his eye-brain connections work but if you do not put extra pressure on him when he is afraid, he is more able to think his way through the challenging situation. This ability to stop and think can be encouraged in a horse if you allow him to do just that: stop and work it out!

Here you can see our little pony Ricky traveling through a narrow gap. If you study the photo sequence, I think you'll be able to answer the following question.

Which side of the gap is scary to Ricky?

1 NARROW SPACES

Passing through narrow spaces.

A horse that rushes through narrow spaces can put the handler, the rider, and anyone around them in danger of being trapped and crushed. Think of the number of doorways, gates, and corridors you travel through with your horse: each one has the potential to cause anxiety in your horse because he feels trapped. It's worth helping him get used to this so that you can feel safe when these claustrophobic situations arise.

In the photo below, the truck and the bank with a fence on top create a neat gap for us to practice.

The truck and the bank-and-fence create the kind of narrow gap you might face any old day at home, at a show, or on the trail.

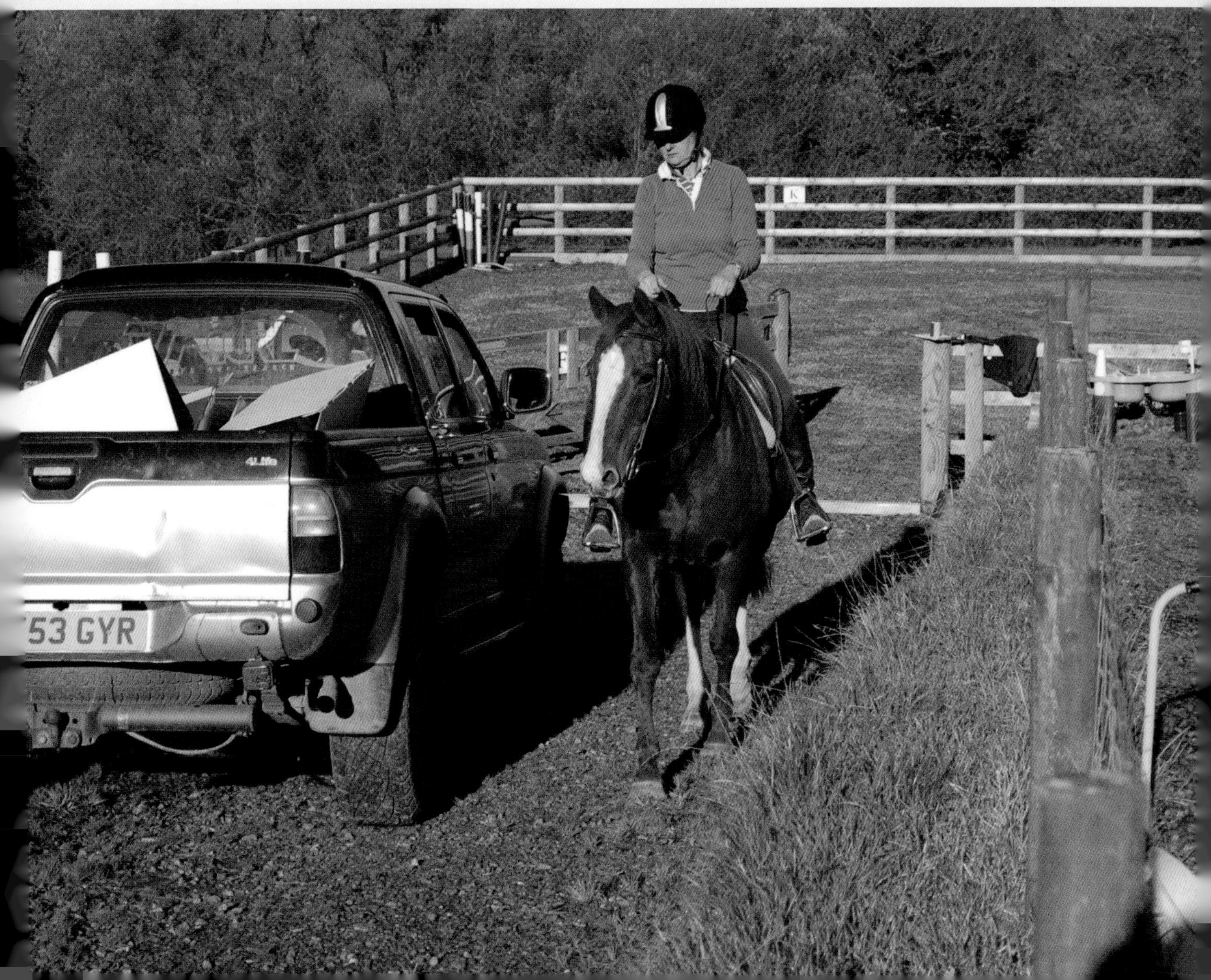

Exercise 1 · Narrow Spaces

A I like to start with two plastic barrels to create a safe gap. You may need to have the barrels farther apart to start. Ask the horse to wait.

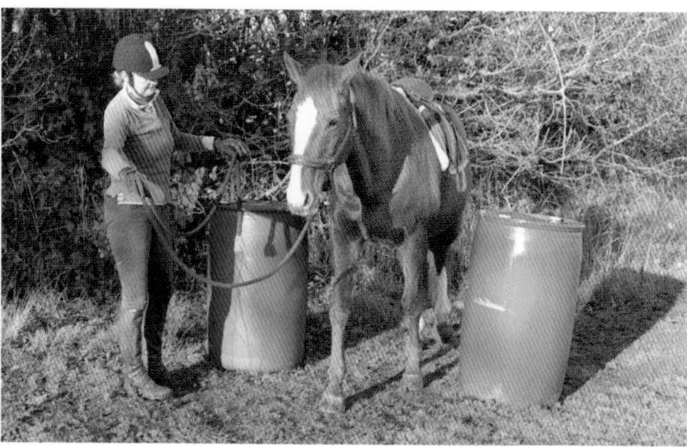

B Walk through the barrels while the horse stands still, then invite him to join you.

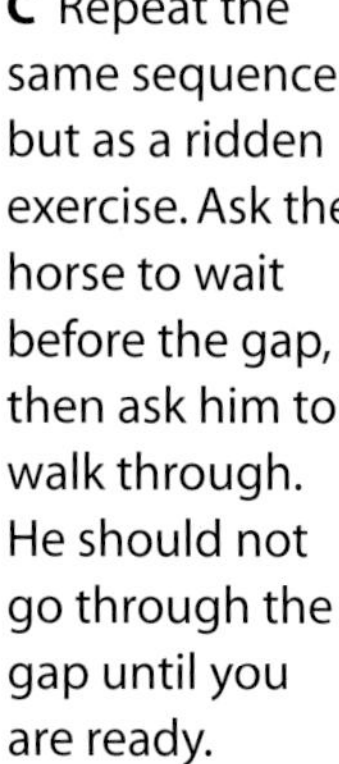

C Repeat the same sequence but as a ridden exercise. Ask the horse to wait before the gap, then ask him to walk through. He should not go through the gap until you are ready.

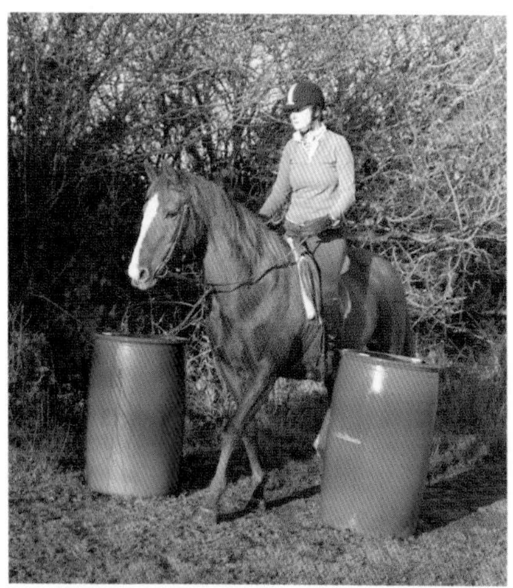

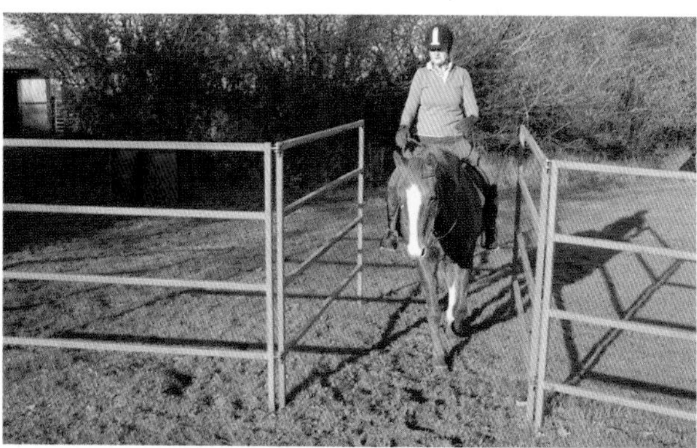

D Find another type of narrow gap and make sure the horse knows not to rush through, which could endanger your legs when riding.

E We take for granted that a horse finds walking in and out of a stall easy but for some that narrow doorway can cause real problems.

F Never allow your horse to rush through a gateway. It is very easy for your legs to get caught on all the hooks and hinges.

G On the way out of the arena, the gateway and the space between the truck and the bank form a narrow gap for us to practice our skills.

H On a ride in the wood, we find a natural gap to ride through.

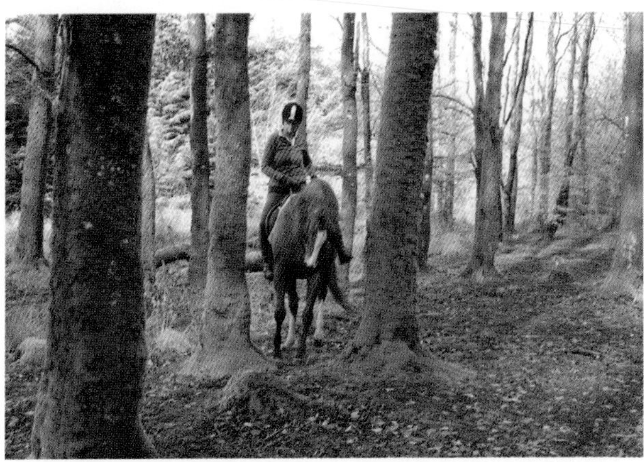

I My horse decides she will hurry through it. I will do whatever I need to do to protect myself even if it looks ugly!

J I quietly reposition her. You can see by her ears that she is concerned about our previous conversation.

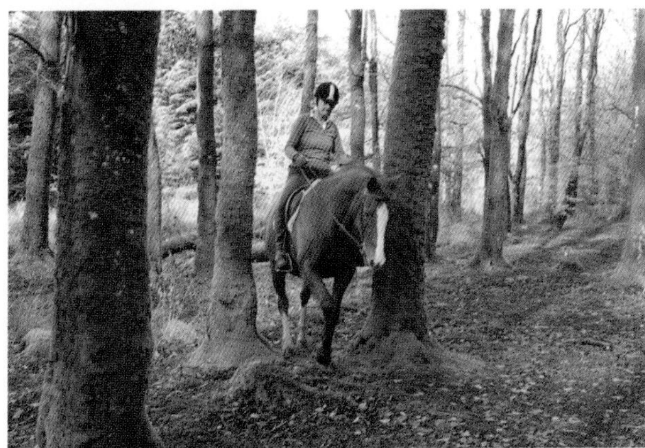

K Then I allow her to flow through.

L I'm reassuring her that her mistake is forgotten and all is well.

2 THE POLE CORRIDOR

Helping a horse cope with the pressure of a pole corridor.

Before I started really looking in detail at obstacles and how horses react to them, I never appreciated just how much pressure a horse can feel from a pole on the ground. Horses that have never been hit with poles or trapped between them can be as sensitive as those who have. These horses often find it difficult to stand in a trailer or stall because the "pressure" of the walls on both sides can worry them.

Sometimes walls and enclosed spaces put "pressure" on a horse; preparing for this helps him remain calm and accepting.

Exercise 2 · The Pole Corridor

A Place two poles on the ground about 10 feet (3m) apart and lead your horse through them at walk.

B Keep walking through until the horse is totally relaxed about it, then ask him to stop for one second before walking on. Increase the wait until he is happy to stand between the two poles for as long as you ask.

C Now start to place the poles closer together, making the corridor narrower.

D Keep bringing the poles closer; here the distance between them is 18 inches (about 50cm) apart.

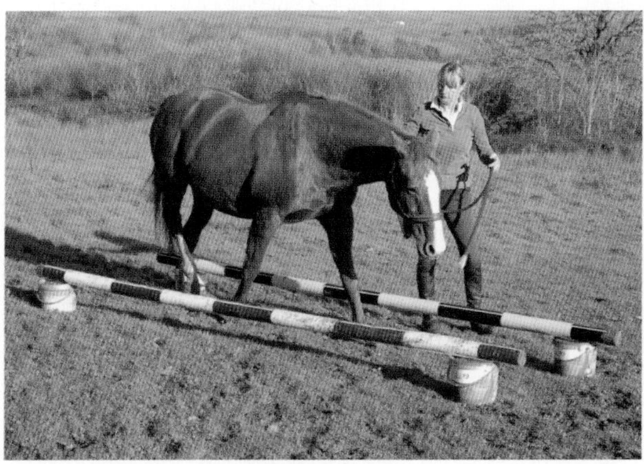

E You can lift the sides a little.

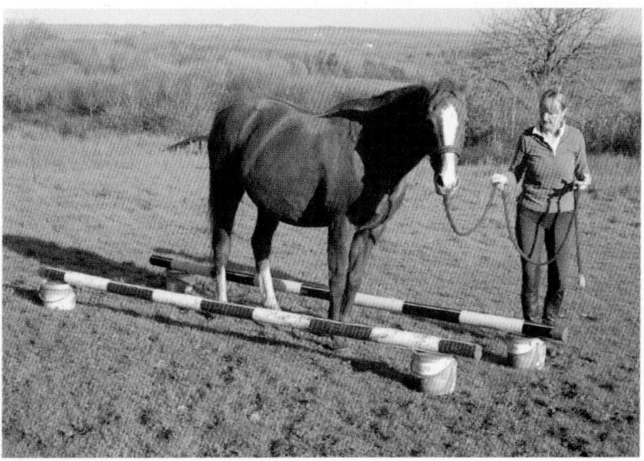

F As he becomes more confident, you can ask him to stand for longer periods.

3 THE START BOX

Learning to wait in the start box on a cross-country course—but being ready to go when asked.

To keep a horse calm and focused before a competition takes a lot of discipline and practice by the rider so that her nerves do not affect the horse. It's always a shame when a horse runs out of energy halfway round a course because he's lost so much energy just waiting his turn at the gate.

A surefire way to bring your anxiety down (and therefore your horse's too) is practice. Many cross-country courses are available for private hire and if you can just go and play around the obstacles with no pressure, you and your horse will become familiar with them and have few surprises on competition day.

The first obstacle is the Start Box, so often neglected as a place to train yourself and your horse to be disciplined and quiet, but well worth doing because you don't want to run out of energy before the end. The horse needs to wait quietly and not burn up valuable energy waiting to go.

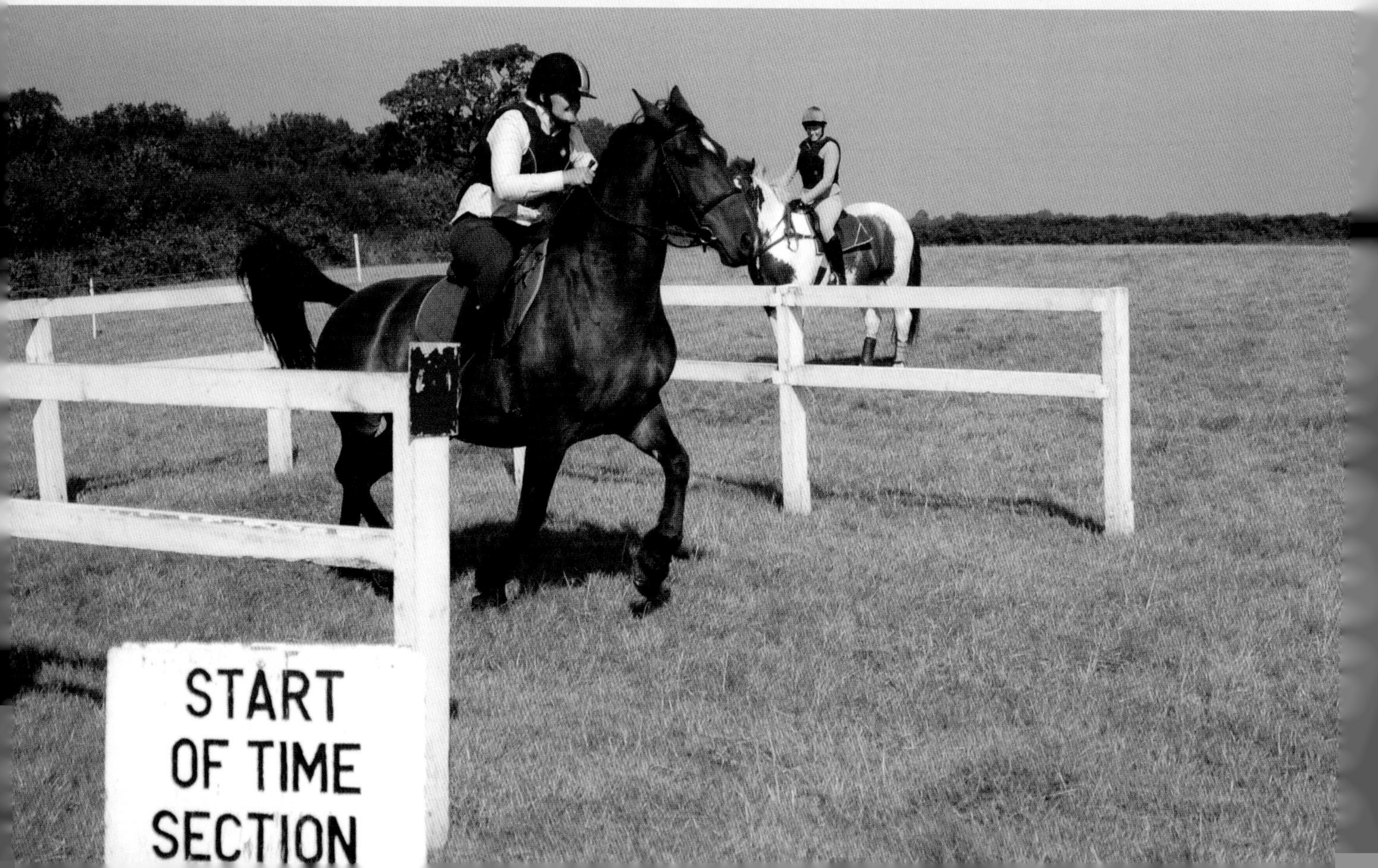

There are often exciting "starts" to group rides or competitions, such as the start box in cross-country, where a horse needs to learn to wait quietly and not burn up valuable energy.

Exercise 3 · The Start Box

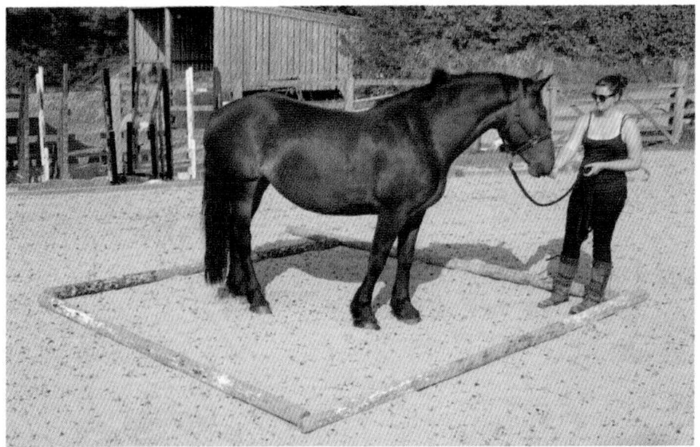

A Start with a pole "box," and ensure the horse is comfortable both with standing still and moving through it before you go on.

B Remove the front of the pole box and walk, then trot the horse out.

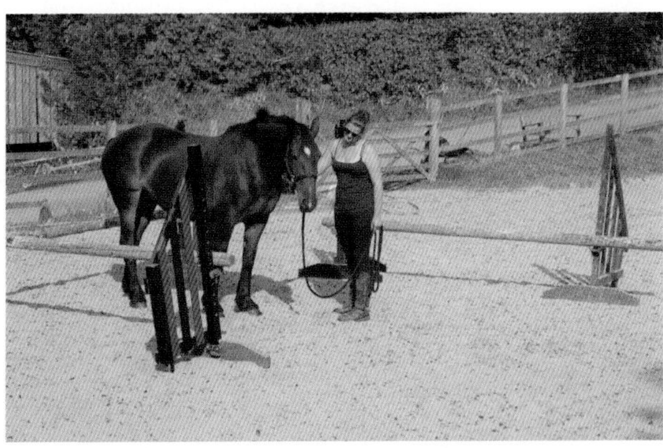

C Lift the "box" until the horse is comfortable standing in it.

D Walk out of the box and build up to trotting out of it.

E Move the horse around the box, stopping, starting, and turning so that the horse gets used to staying in the box without always rushing out.

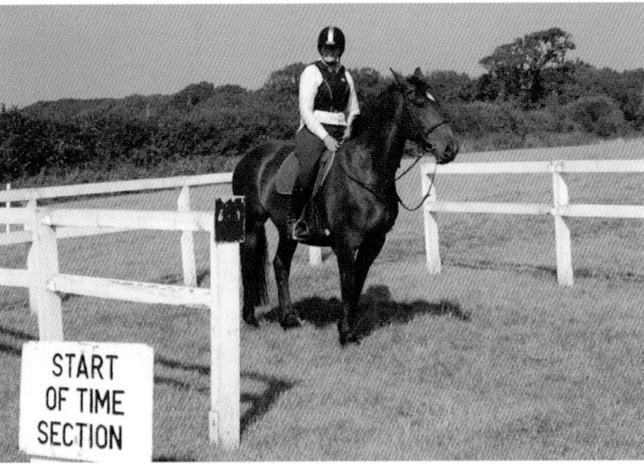

F The horse should wait quietly before being asked to leave at whatever pace you want.

"Sound Advice"

All Fours

Here's a bit of fun and a chance for you to feel what it is like to have four legs. Find somewhere comfortable and get down on all fours. Be careful if you have physical issues such as a bad back or shoulder as you may have to put a little effort into trying to move like a horse.

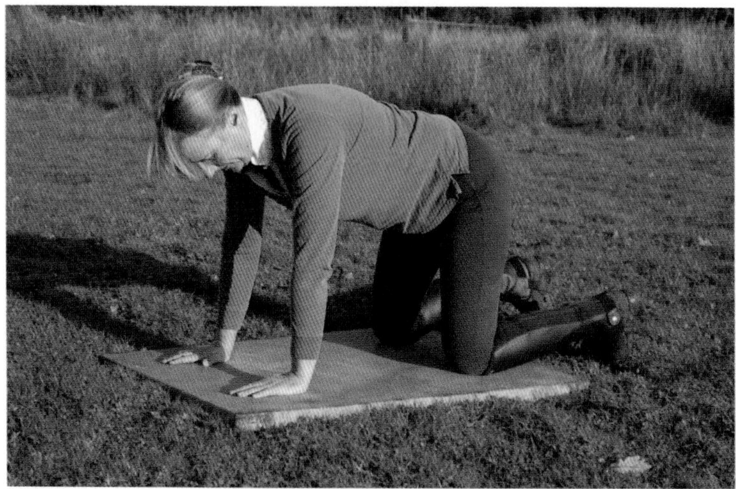

A On all fours make sure that you have a leg at each corner like a table, with your hands under your shoulders and your knees under your hips. This is how a young horse stands.

B Now you are going to try and lift your forehand, in other words, rear like a horse. You will find you have to drop down first to have the energy to push up, using your arms to lift your upper body off the ground.

C You will probably find you use one arm more than the other to help you lift off the ground. Watch young horses playing in the pasture and you will see they do this.

D Rearing, with a leg at each corner like this, is hard work. If you want your horse to be light on the forehand you need to think about what he physically needs to do to achieve it.

E Start again, but this time bring one of your legs forward, placing your knee on the ground under your belly button.

F Now when you lift the forehand it should feel easy because you have a knee to balance over and help lift up the front.

G Now put yourself into the shape of a collected horse with both your knees forward under your belly.

H You will find the forehand becomes very light and easy to lift, which is what we call being "light on the forehand" when we ride.

4 GATES

Safely negotiating opening and closing gates.

I always say to my students that if you can open and close a gate calmly and efficiently while riding your horse, you're a long way to being in control of your horse's feet. Just think of all the different ways you need to move those feet and all while holding the reins in one hand if you don't want to let go of the gate.

Because there is more than one type of gate in the world, you may need to practice opening gates towards and away from you, and leaning down to reach a catch or move a lever. I cannot stress how complete this exercise is and a great test of where you are in your horsemanship. I put this and easy trailer loading of my horses at the top of my list of things I want to be able to do calmly and easily.

All gates are different, some opening towards you and some away, while others have walls or hedges alongside them. You need to adapt some of the movements below to complete the task with a different type of gate.

You should never have to dismount to open, go through, and shut a gate behind you.

A gate should be a quiet place. When it causes anxiety in you or the horse, it can become very difficult to open and close while on horseback.

Exercise 4 · Gates

A Walk through the process of opening and closing a gate without the horse.

B You will need to be able to go forward.

C Stop and go back.

D You need to be able to move the front end over, a turn-on-the-forehand (see *Blueprint 5*, p. 17).

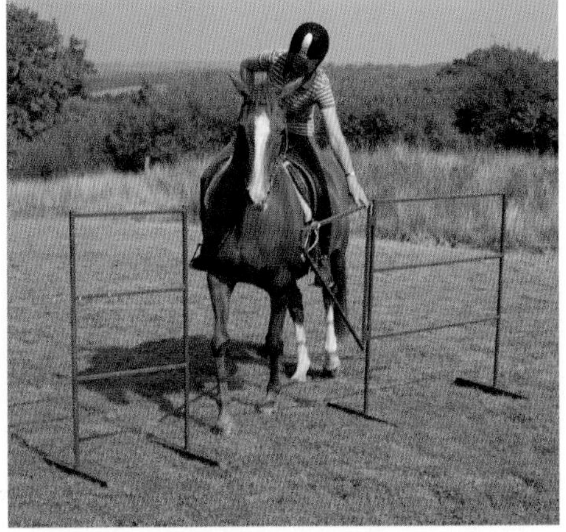

E You need to be able to move the hind end over (see *Blueprint 4*, p. 14).

F Approach the gate quietly, setting up the right position before you reach the gate.

Exercise 4 · Gates (cont.)

G Unlatch the gate and open it by turning the forehand in towards the gate.

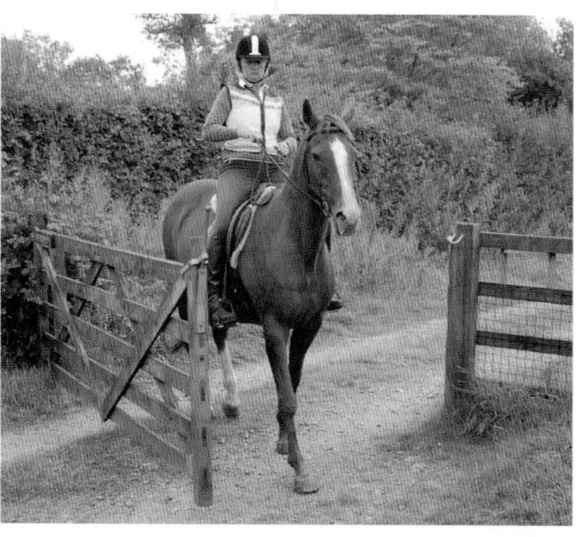

H The horse must wait before passing through the gap. Here, he is rushing through.

I The horse is just about to step over with the hindquarters.

J Close the gate by moving the horse over sideways, or just the forehand.

5 TRAFFIC

Learning to accept vehicles on the road.

When you think of a horse working to a risk assessment that was designed so many years ago, you can completely understand why a vehicle traveling towards him at speed would cause him to run. If he's not seen traffic before, it's unlikely he's going to stand still. Nature made horses so that they run first and ask questions later. Those that stopped and considered the situation died out.

So the answer is not to start with a fast-moving vehicle. Start with a stationary one and build up slowly until the car is traveling quite fast. If your horse is afraid it may not be the actual vehicle causing it: the sound, or the smell of the person inside could also be the cause. Isolate each of these before you assume it is just the moving vehicle. There is no quick fix to helping horses accept that traffic will not harm them: it takes time and patience—without creating such a challenging situation that the horse goes into flight.

Horses should be prepared to face all kinds of shapes, styles, and sizes of vehicles, and in close quarters.

Exercise 5 · Traffic

A Make sure it is the traffic and not just the sights and sounds of the road.

B The combination of the street with its white lines, phone booths, and signs may already have your horse on alert. A moving car just might tip him into flight mode.

C It may be a particular type of vehicle, such as a noisy motorbike that worries him.

D If your horse does not like going through narrow gaps, this truck could cause a problem for him.

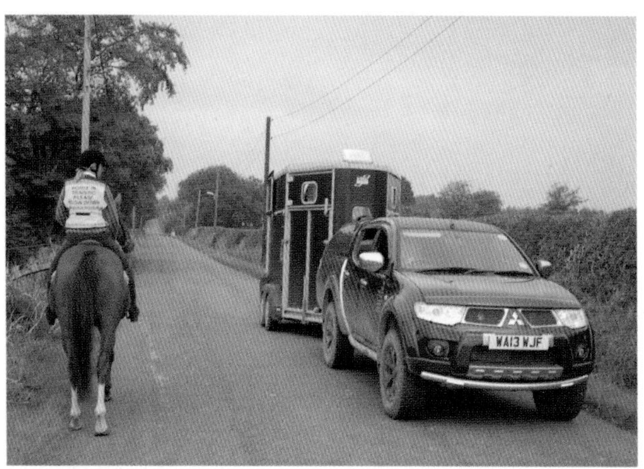

E This horse trailer stopped and gave us plenty of room; other vehicles may not do this for you.

F This large tractor was not only very noisy but smelly too.

G So how do you help the horse? Well, start with just a small vehicle with no one in it: no engine running, just a car. Let the horse inspect the vehicle and see that it is safe.

H Now move away and ask someone to start the engine and leave the car running. Let the horse hear and smell the car.

I Ask someone to drive the car forward and backward so the horse can see that it changes shape and the noise varies.

J Ask the car to drive past you with you going in the opposite direction, then you turn and "chase" the car away. I find this to be the most powerful way of putting a horse in control of the situation.

K As your horse becomes more accustomed he can be helped to face the oncoming vehicle.

L The speed, sound, and size of the vehicle can start to change, but do be very careful that your helper, who is driving, knows that when you call "Stop!" you mean it. That's why we do this before we go because you may not have this option on the real road.

"Sound Advice"

Why a Horse Says, "No," and How He Might Say It

How often do you hear someone describe a horse as "stubborn" or "clever?" Quite often, I expect.

My observations have shown me that when a horse is called "stubborn," it is because he has outwitted a human; and those horses who are called "clever" are the ones that make the human feel good about themselves.

I haven't met a stubborn horse for years and all the horses I meet are clever!

A horse will do one of four things to stay alive.

- Flight—first choice: if there's an exit he'll take it.
- Freeze—when he really doesn't know what to do, he will just stand still.
- Fight—when all escape routes are blocked and the thing that's scaring him is in the way, he'll fight it.
- Faint—he'll collapse because in his mind all hope is lost.

Our aim as horse handlers is to never put the horse in the position where he needs to employ one of these four 'F's. If a horse does not do what we want we need to ask ourselves why.

- Is it because he's in pain?
- Is he afraid?
- Is he tired?
- Does he not believe in his handler?
- Or does he just not understand the question?

Once you start to analyze why a horse does or does not do what you want, you always find that he is just looking for a way to survive—a way to peace.

By changing your attitude, you could well start to meet a lot of very "clever" horses just trying to work with you to find the path to peace.

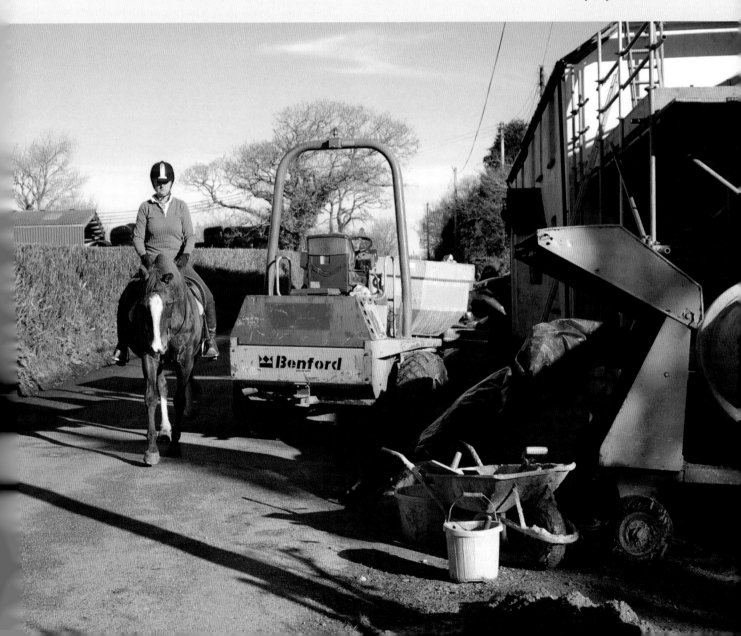

6 ROAD WORKS AND CONSTRUCTION

Riding and walking safely past construction sites.

As always when riding on the road, you need to be considerate of other road users so for this exercise you will need to simulate road works at home first. Training your horse to accept construction both on and beside the road is imperative since the general public often assumes horses are bombproof. As you know this can never be 100 percent but you can go a long way to making things safer for everyone. Drivers often don't have the patience to wait for you to calm your horse down sufficiently to pass the road works and that's when accidents happen.

A construction site is full of potentially scary objects.

Exercise 6 · Road Works and Construction

A You will need a collection of road signs, cones, hazard tape, wheelbarrows, in fact anything that you might find on a construction site. Please be aware that it is dangerous—and illegal—to remove these without permission, construction workers' safety may be put at risk if you do.

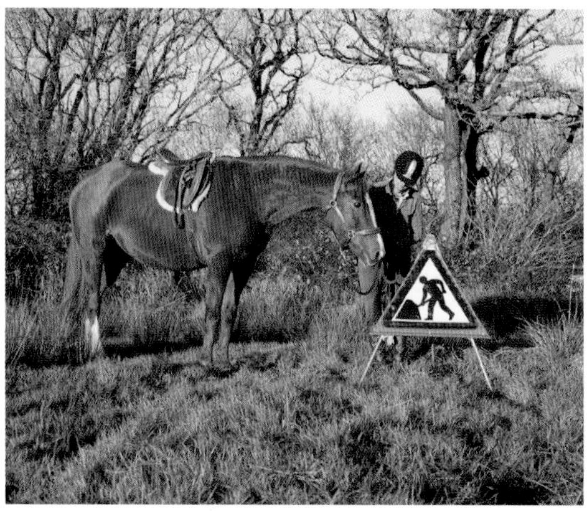

B Start on the ground with one item and allow the horse to explore it.

C Make sure you are next to the scary object as you walk past so that the horse does not jump onto you.

D Introduce other items to increase the challenge for the horse.

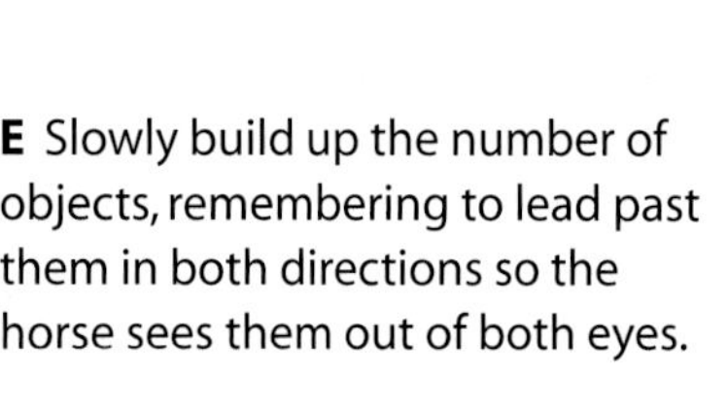

E Slowly build up the number of objects, remembering to lead past them in both directions so the horse sees them out of both eyes.

F Create a corridor of a few items and lead the horse through it.

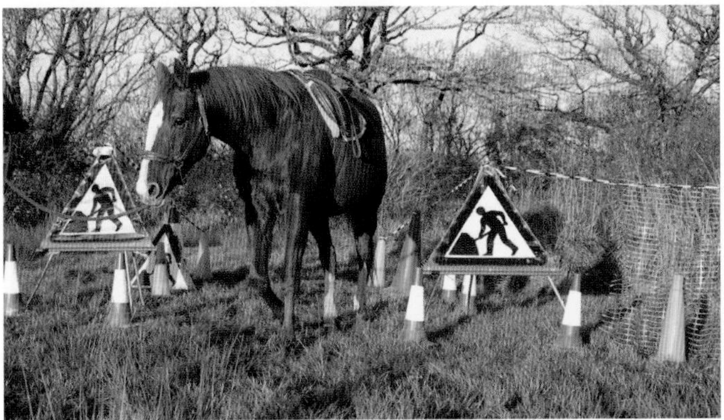

G It's a good idea to let your horse find his own way through so he is not just following you. When you ride he may not have the confidence to do it without you being in front.

H When you start to ride through, go back to the beginning with one object.

I Build the challenge by adding more objects closer together, creating a narrow gap with items on both sides.

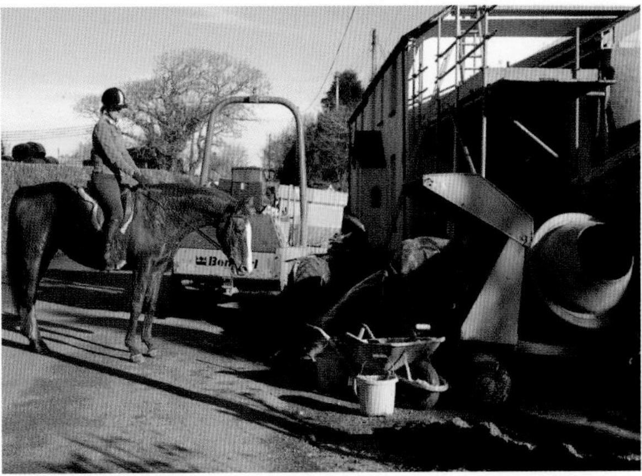

J Whenever possible let the horse stop and look to satisfy his curiosity.

7 STROLLERS AND PUSHCHAIRS

Understanding that rolling carts are not predators.

I hear more and more horse riders commenting that their horse is truly terrified of strollers. I don't think it's because a stroller is more scary than ever before, I believe it's because the designs are becoming more robust and so able to go "off road" with their bigger wheels and easy-to-push design.

You will need to borrow or obtain a stroller for this exercise and remove the child! Do not use food in the stroller to tempt the horse to investigate; this would not be a good idea once a child is on board. The child and riders in these photographs are all well known to each other. Do not take any risks with this exercise: practicing with an empty stroller is very important as horses may turn and kick or strike out when they are afraid.

You can meet strollers anywhere these days!

Exercise 7 · Strollers and Pushchairs

A Let the horse explore the stroller when it is not moving.

B Do not use food to encourage the horse towards the stroller; one day there may be an infant on board.

C Allow him to see the stroller from all angles.

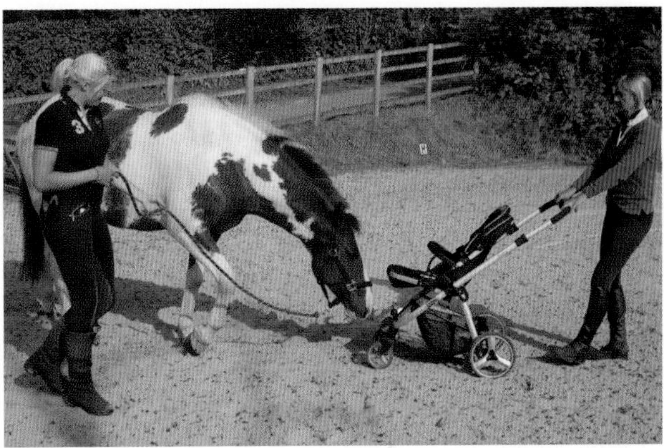

D Let him follow the stroller so that he does not feel it is chasing him.

E Ask someone to push the stroller past him and let him follow it.

F This stroller, complete with child, belongs to the rider of the horse. They have built a safe relationship but do be careful when mixing things up like this.

8 TRASH AND RUBBISH BAGS

Making friends with trash!

Some of my most dramatic "backups" have been initiated by a trash bag parked outside a house. My previous horse, a gray Arabian called Treacle, really needed help with this one as she was convinced they were waiting to pounce on her as she went past. With her I kept it very simple: I delivered her hay in a black bag and the association of food made her look with more interest at the trash bags by the road. Indeed, sometimes she approached with great enthusiasm in the hope that a flake of hay might be inside.

Making friends with garbage trucks and recycling vehicles, their drivers, and their loads is part of this exercise.

Secret and I make friends with a recycling truck and its drivers.

Exercise 8 · Trash and Rubbish Bags

A To a horse a rubbish bag must look horribly like an animal ready to pounce!

B Start with a small bag; do not increase the number until your horse is very comfortable with this.

C Place another bag on the pile…

D …until there is a whole pile of bags.

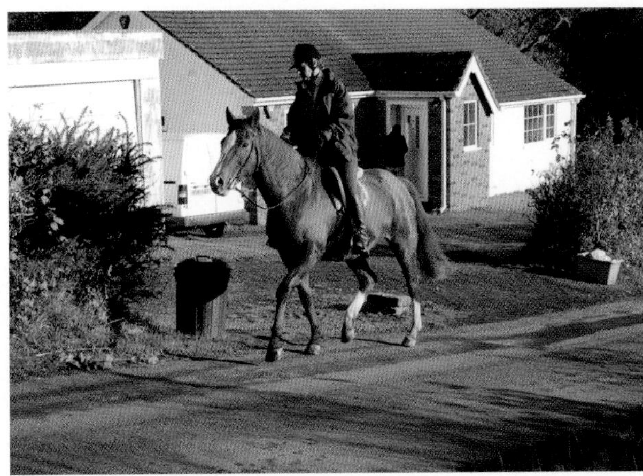

E Trash containers come in lots of shapes and sizes so you may need to borrow some different types of containers to help your horse get used to the various designs.

F Let the horse explore the different shapes and colors at every opportunity.

PIGS

Befriending them.

There are many theories as to why horses don't like pigs. Is it because they are low to the ground, taking on a classic predator shape? Is it their distinctive smell or the grunting noises that may sound like a growl? We could spend hours trying to work out why but actually pigs and horses can live together very happily.

In the New Forest in England, pigs and wild ponies live together in the oak woods. I have seen pet pigs running with horses on summer pastures with no drama at all. Once we have decided what is possible we just need to work out a strategy to make it happen.

On this page, Emma and her horse Maddy greet Pinky and Perky, their neighbor pigs.

Emma and her horse Maddy greet Pinky and Perky.

Exercise 9 · Pigs

A After leading her horse, spiraling towards and away from the pigs using *Advance and Retreat, Blueprint 3* (p. 11), Emma shows the pigs to Maddy.

B Now that he is closer to the pigs, Maddy isn't so sure. Emma stays calm and lets him think.

C Emma doesn't stop Maddy moving as long as he doesn't run into her. She just stays calm and waits for the horse to join her.

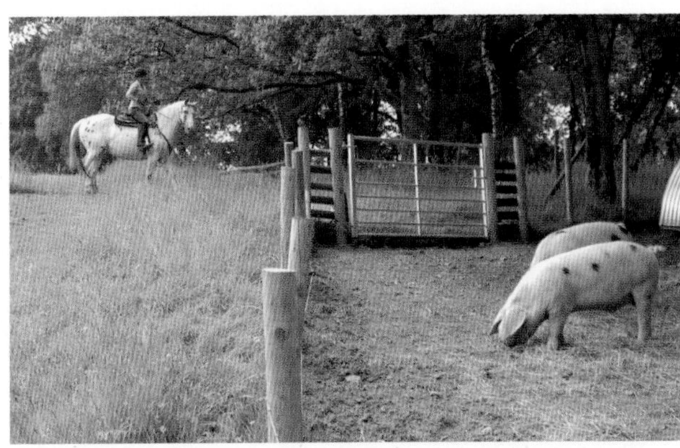

D Once Maddy is happy with Emma on the ground, Emma gets into the saddle and repeats the same spiraling movements of *Advance and Retreat* to get near the pigs again. She does not make a direct approach.

E Emma rides in spirals, circles, and figure eights getting nearer to the pigs…

F …until the horse is able to stand near the pigs.

10 SHEEP

How to accept sheep and even start to "herd" them.

In England, it is rare for people to use horses to move cattle and sheep anymore, but it's a great skill to learn because it really gets the feet of the horse moving, putting all those practice sessions to purpose! The sheep in these pictures are Shetland sheep and behave more like deer than our usual British sheep so Emma and Flynn had to move quietly at the start to prevent them from completely panicking.

Emma and Flynn have a little fun herding some sheep.

Exercise 10 · Sheep

A Emma shows Flynn the sheep. You may need to use *Advance and Retreat* to get this far (p. 11).

B The sheep are released into the field so that Flynn can see how they move. Emma reassures Flynn that all is well.

C Emma begins to move the sheep around so that Flynn can see they are moving away from him rather than likely to chase him.

D Now in the saddle, Emma lets Flynn inspect the sheep as before. You can see he feels slightly different about them now Emma is no longer on the ground beside him.

E With Emma and Flynn standing well to one side, the sheep are released and travel away from the horse, which gives Flynn time to think.

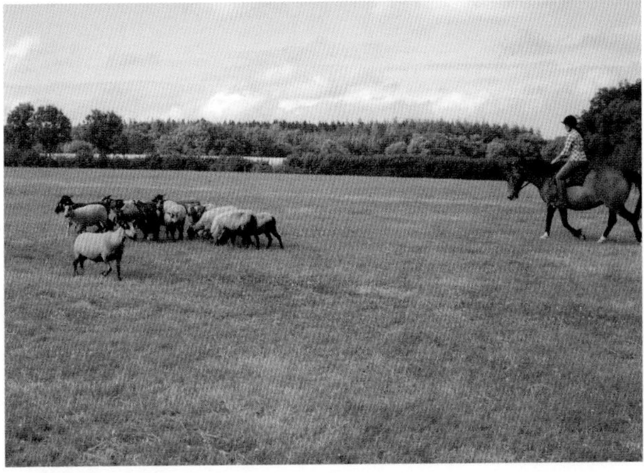

F Emma and Flynn quietly start moving the sheep.

11 PLASTIC-COVERED BALES

Accepting "marshmallows."

You would think that a horse recognizes food when he sees it but not when it is wrapped up in colored plastic!

When we first started delivering our black plastic-covered bales with a tractor—with the bale impaled on a spike 10 feet in the air so it can be dropped into the horse-feeding ring—there was pandemonium among our horses. But within a few weeks our problem was reversed as we had to try and keep the horses away so that we could safely install the bale into the feeder. Eventually we had to fence them out at delivery time. That pleasant association of the tractor bringing food helped in other ways too: none of our horses is scared by a tractor now because it is bringing food.

You never know what you might meet on the trail: it is common to pass fields with stacks of "marshmallows," or old bales lining or dumped in a lane.

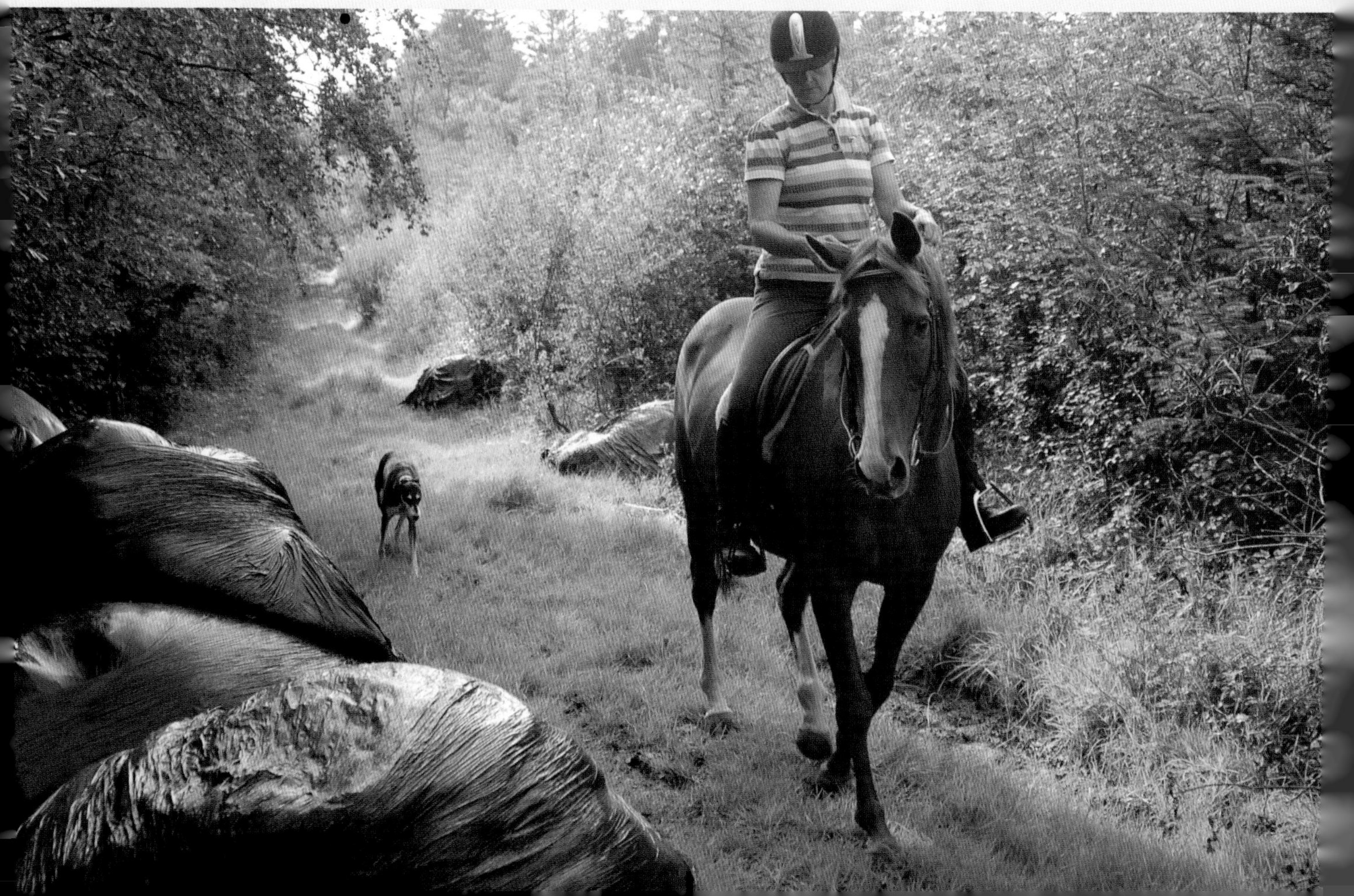

Round bales and "marshmallows" can appear anywhere!

Exercise 11 · Plastic-Covered Bales

A Let the horse inspect the bale.

B Now give him a job to do and play around the bale.

C Once you are in the saddle, show the bale to the horse. You may need to use *Advance and Retreat* tactics here if he is really not sure (see *Blueprint 3*, p. 11).

D Ride around the black bale so that the horse can see it out of both eyes and notice that its shape changes as we move around it.

E Not all bales are wrapped in plastic but they can still cause some anxiety at first sight.

F Here the bales are piled up. Let the horse stop and look. Do not force him to go near them; let him move backward and forward to look at them in different ways as he satisfies himself that they are safe.

12 FLAPPING FESTIVE DECORATIONS

Staying calm around bunting.

With health and safety at horse shows becoming more and more of an issue, the areas where horses and the general public can pass are often marked out using lines of small flags or hazard tape. Commonly, these are arranged in corridors so that the horse moving between the vehicle lot and the show ring becomes one long road edged by flapping plastic. By the time the horse has reached the ring he can be so frightened he cannot compete at his best, but it is very simple to help the horse at home and in his own environment to realize that lines of flags are not dangerous and have nothing to do with him.

Once you have accustomed your horse to flags and festive plastic items, riding through a "flapping" corridor is easy.

Once your horse is used to strings of flapping flags, riding past them at a horse show or on the trail is easy.

Exercise 12 · Flapping Festive Decorations

A Start with one line of flags at nose level and let your horse look.

B Lead your horse past the decorations, making sure that you are between the horse and it because if he spooks, he will jump away from you.

C As you gain confidence that your horse is not going to spook into you, you can swap sides and have the horse between you and the decorative items.

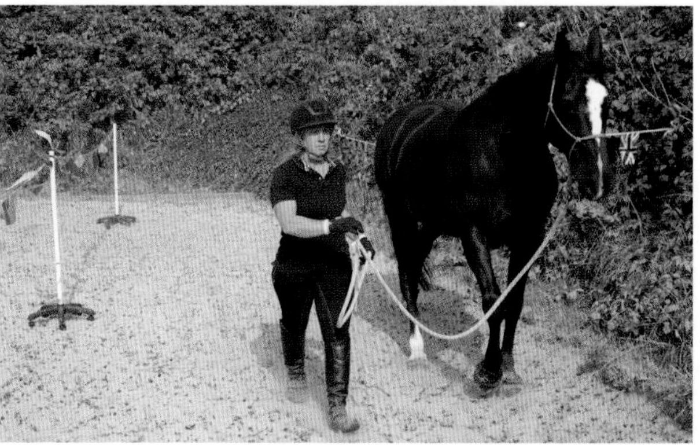

D Now create a wide corridor with flags and festive items on both sides and lead your horse through it.

E Make the corridor slowly more narrow.

F Now you are going to ride. Make the corridor wide to start with then slowly make it narrower as before.

13 SMOKE

Riding through and being around smoke.

When I started the Horse Agility Club some people asked me (not always seriously) whether I would be jumping my horse through fire. My family motto happens to be "Why not?"—so I immediately set to work to find out how to do this safely. After some research and experimentation I found that the fire was not the problem but the smoke was what caused anxiety to the horse. The unpredictable nature of the swirling cloud of smoke that preceded the flames was enough to scare most horses.

I began to think of other instances when horses might have to negotiate smoke in a domestic environment. The hot shoeing of horses, cattle branding, and just riding along and encountering a garden bonfire with smoke blowing across the road are times when a horse needs to be aware that it is not dangerous. I've never found the smell of smoke to be a problem but the sight certainly can cause quite a reaction.

"Smoking" is not good for your health!

Exercise 13 · Smoke

A Respect your horse's fear. It is genuine; fires can be dangerous. We used paper and damp leaves to create the smoke. These flames very quickly died away.

B Let the horse look at the smoke. If you need to, use *Advance and Retreat* methods to get here.

C A lot of horses will have seen this before when being hot shod.

D When there is a thin stream of smoke, lead your horse through, making sure that you are in a safe position.

E You can start to ride around the smoke, taking advantage of the moments it moves in your direction. To be sure your horse does not spook from the smoke and into the fire, keep your distance from it.

F Eventually my horse stood while the smoke billowed around us.

14 BUSHES

Pushing through a noodle wall then a thick bush.

We spend all our time helping our horse to understand that he needs to give to pressure rather than push into it so he can become a little confused when we ask him to push through something that may appear solid to him. When you think about it, the only time we ask the horse to push into the pressure is when we get on, and when we drive him in a cart and ask him to push into the collar.

So it takes a lot of trust for a horse to break the rule and push through a barrier. It can help to put a vocal cue in here such as "Push" so the horse knows what is required. I use the same cue when I ask him to push a ball with his nose. This gives him confidence that he is doing the right thing. If you are riding he needs to know that you really do mean it when you ask him to push forward.

Remember, too, that he may not be able to see the surface below the items he is being asked to push through so this exercise requires tact and patience. You also need to observe when the horse is giving the slightest attempt to try so you can give copious praise to encourage him that you are there to support him.

You will need five or six soft foam "pool noodles" and a way of attaching them to uprights such as jump wings or panels. We simply tied lengths of pipe insulation to our round-pen panels.

When well prepared with practice through a noodle wall, thick brush like this is no problem.

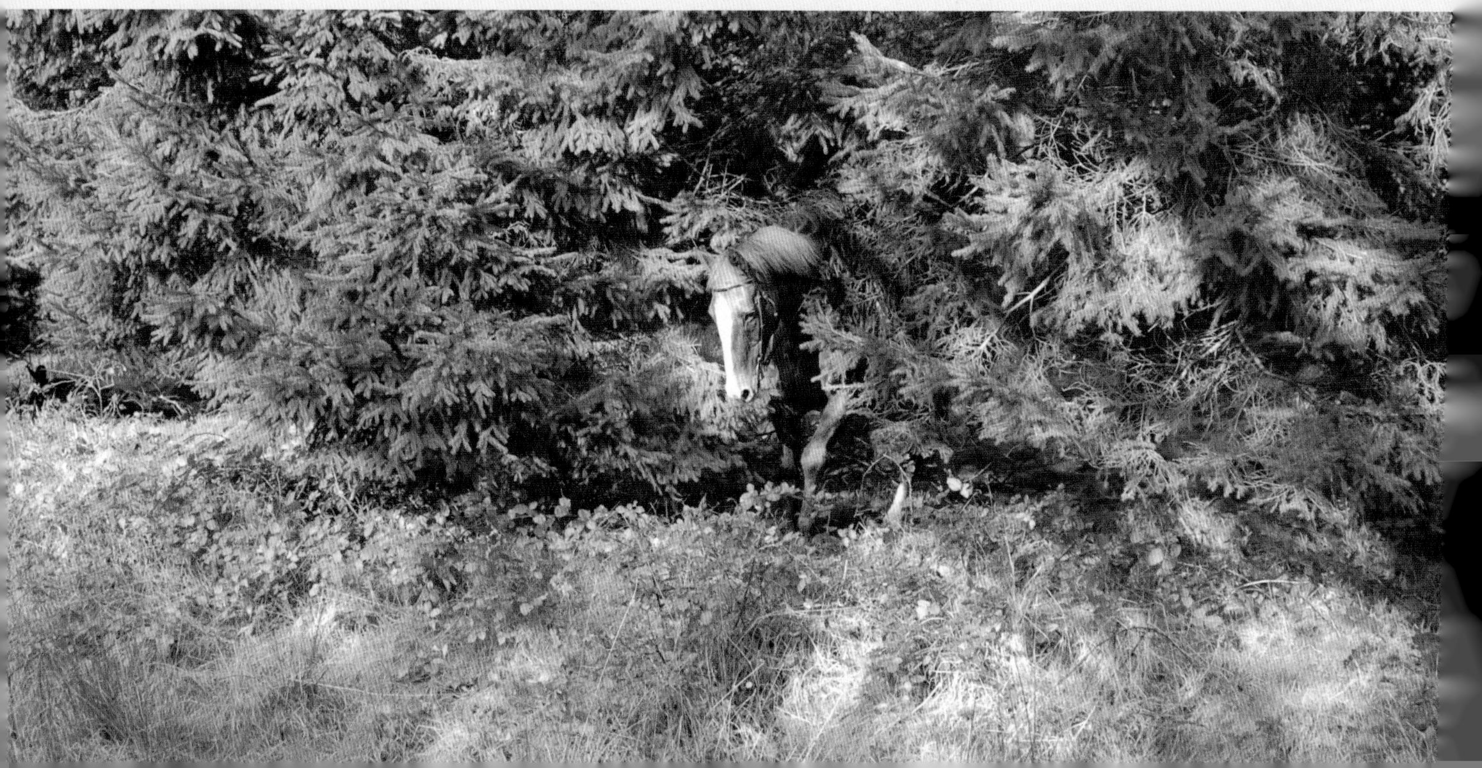

Exercise 14 • Bushes

A Let the horse inspect the noodle using *Advance and Retreat*. Rub the noodle across his chest and along his body.

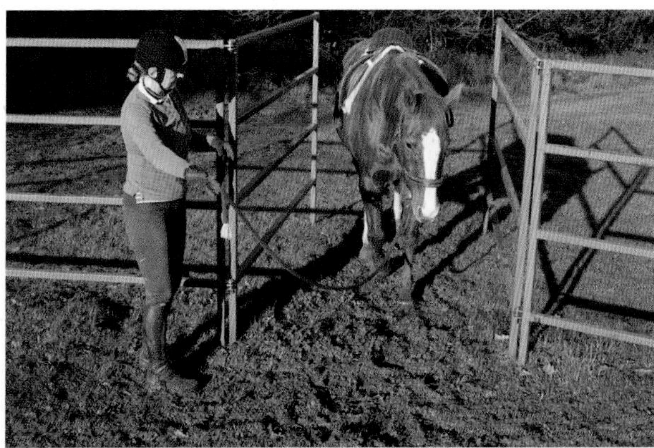

B Make sure the horse is able to pass through the gap without the noodles.

C With only one or two noodles only, lead him against the noodle. He may be concerned about this because he has been trained not to push into pressure.

D Increase the number of noodles. You may do this on the ground or when riding, whatever you and your horse are ready for.

E Let your horse stop and think about this: it looks very solid but if you have slowly built up the number of noodles, he will negotiate them one by one.

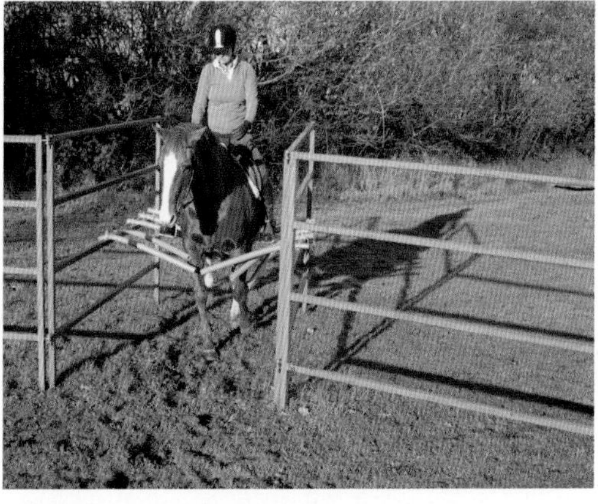

F Increase the number of noodles and decrease the distance between them until the horse is confidently pushing through.

15 PLASTIC BOTTLES

Wading through a pool of plastic bottles.

I had seen pictures of horses wading through ball pools in Western Trail competitions but discovered that the balls used in children's play areas were not only quite fragile under the weight of a horse but expensive to buy in the quantities I would need to give a reasonable depth.

On looking around my local recycling center my eye caught sight of a big net full of plastic bottles. Light, with no sharp edges, these are ideal to create a pool of bottles deep enough for a horse to wade through. By saving these at home, and asking friends and family to help, you can quickly build up quite a collection. Make sure they are well washed out (otherwise they can get smelly and attract insects) and only use bottles that have contained food stuff, not household cleaners of any kind. I remove the lids on mine but it is not absolutely necessary as long as the horse is not allowed to chew the bottles and perhaps swallow a lid.

Wading through a deep pit of bottles teaches your horse to be calm with things around and under his feet.

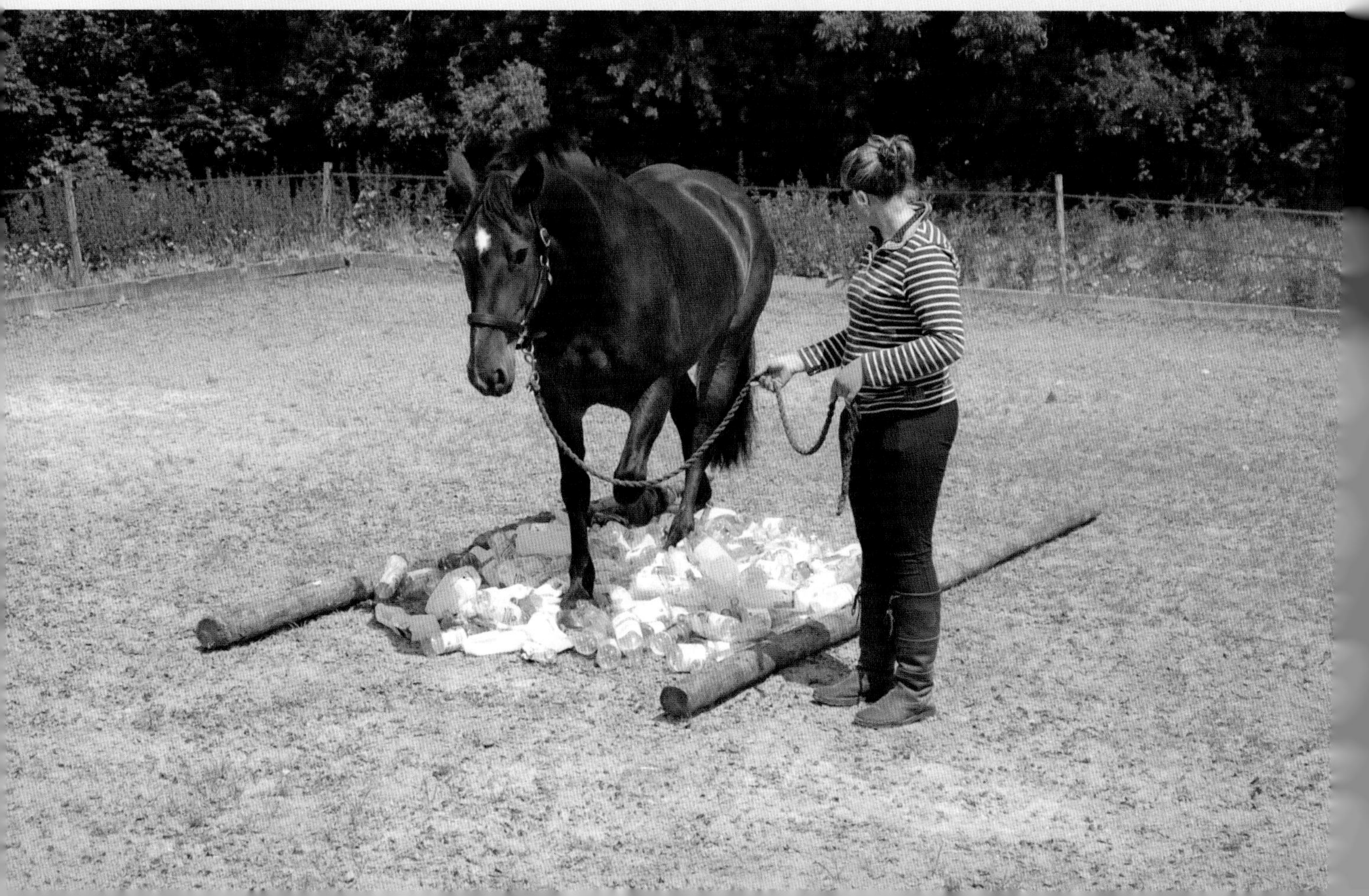

Exercise 15 · Plastic Bottles

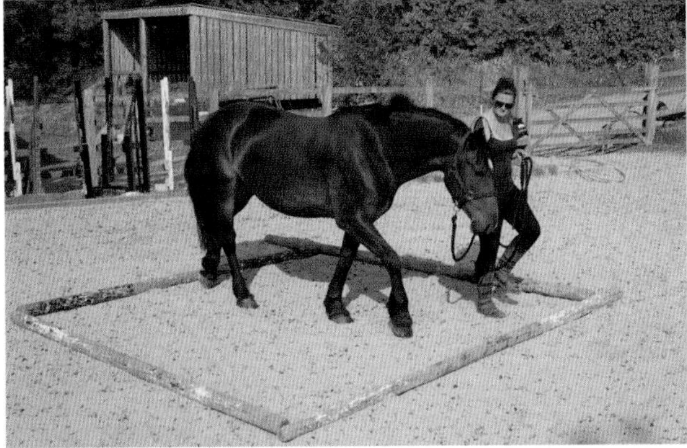

A Create a pole frame on the ground and lead your horse through to make sure he is comfortable with that part of the exercise.

B You will need a collection of plastic bottles with no lids and no labels. Lead or ride your horse through the frame with one bottle.

C As he becomes confident, add more and more bottles.

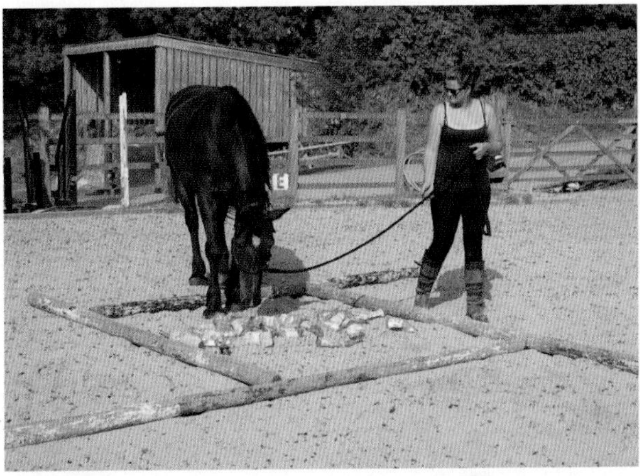

D The horse will confidently wade through the bottles once he has been allowed to satisfy himself that it is safe.

E Walk him through until he no longer needs to check out the safety of the obstacle.

F Once he is comfortable you can halt in the bottles or trot through them.

16 DRESSAGE BOARDS

Ignoring arena markers.

It is such a disappointment when you enter a competition having trained hard and polished your horse and your skills only to lose valuable marks because your horse becomes fixated on something as simple as a white dressage-arena edging board. But this is something that easily can be worked on in the safety of your own home arena or paddock, and you don't even need to purchase dressage boards to do it. You can use white poles or plumbing pipe to simulate the effect of the white edges to a dressage arena. I use corrugated plastic advertising boards that stores put outside to advertise one-off events then throw away. Many people are very happy to give them to you. All you do is turn the boards inside out and there you have a dressage-edging board. They can be used to create many different obstacles such as mazes and small jumps so it's worth looking out for the next sale at your local stores.

Dressage boards and ring dividers should be introduced gradually, so they don't surprise your horse during a lesson, clinic, or competition.

Exercise 16 · Dressage Boards

A Here you can see me starting to fold my free advertising board into a dressage board.

B I fold the advertisement to the inside.

C I like my horse to be with me as much as possible when I am building obstacles; it's all part of our training process. You may need to look at *Blueprint 3: Advance and Retreat* (p. 11) to help you here.

D If you want to start on the ground, that's fine. This photo shows me riding past one board in the arena. I rode in circles and figure-eights in both directions to get there.

E Slowly increase the number of boards. Remember to ride past in both directions. If your horse is still looking at the board or shies from it, you have gone too fast.

F Put dressage boards or something similar along paths and tracks that the horse travels regularly so seeing this strange object in a new place becomes normal.

17 WIDE OPEN SPACES

Riding safely outside the arena.

And so I reach the last exercise and it's really the reason why I decided to write this book. I want people to ride safely outside the arena because it is so much fun. The sight of a horse and rider galloping freely over open country is a joyful thing of which we all want to be a part. Now the time has come to slowly and safely make this happen. Do not feel under pressure to go outside too soon. One day you will know that the time is right. That first ride can be a short walk out and back: do not feel this is too little; it may be just what you need to take the next step.

Fear is fear, whether it's sky diving or cantering in an open space. One is not more valid than the other, it is just fear. Slowly push that fear in front of you, stretching the comfort zone. Don't get into the flight zone because there is absolutely no reason to do this; in fact, it doesn't help you achieve your goals.

What a terrific feeling!

Feeling confident to canter freely across an open space is a wonderful feeling.

Exercise 17 · Wide Open Spaces

A You may want to start in an arena to give yourself confidence. Don't worry if you have to do this, it's just the first step on the journey: some riders feel vulnerable just riding across the diagonal of the arena because they like to feel supported by the fence.

B Riding along clearly defined roads and tracks will give you confidence to start with. Here you can see the wilds of Dartmoor in the distance, 365 square miles of riding country just waiting to be explored.

C You can progress to less well-defined tracks with no fences.

D Your first ride off a path may be just riding a short way into an open field, turning and going back out again. This little excursion into bigger and bigger spaces means you are not over facing yourself or your horse.

E Eventually you will feel brave enough to explore away from paths and tracks…

F …and choose to take a more interesting, challenging route!

"Sound Advice"

Change One Thing

Deciding to help your horse to become braver out on the trail can look like a daunting task as he spooks at a tiny bird hopping out of the hedge. Suddenly, all those "What ifs?" come crowding in. Now is the time to make a change: not a huge change but one small thing, then another and another, and so on. A lot of small changes can grow into something enormous when they are carefully planned.

So look at each new challenge and think about how you can achieve it then build a safe plan that you feel capable of sticking to and following. First choose your goal. It can be anything from riding a dressage test in an arena to galloping up a mountainside. Just simply decide what you want to do. Think of someone who has already realized this goal and find a picture of that person achieving it if you can. Now place it somewhere where you can see it regularly and feel inspired. After Roger Bannister ran the first four-minute mile, which everyone had said was impossible, other runners—within the very same year—were able to achieve the same result because someone else had shown them it could be done.

Let's pick an example so that I can show you how to build your own Success Map.

Riding Over a Teeter-Totter

First make a list of all the skills you will need to be able to do this.

1 You need to be able to ride your horse and direct his feet.

2 You need to make sure he can cross a tarpaulin, then a wooden board, then maybe walk up onto and over a podium.

3 He may need to become confident walking along a bridge or changes of surface.

Continue writing this list, filling in all the skills you might need to complete the task. Put them in order from easiest to more difficult.

You see the list may be quite long but some of those skills will take seconds, others slightly longer. Notice we do not start with a teeter-totter; we go back to where we are absolutely sure of success and build on that by gradually increasing the challenge as we work.

By starting at the beginning and building up the skills in thin layers, when there is something that doesn't quite work, it is quickly and easily mended by going back a step and reinforcing the previous task. You might be thinking "big" but by doing "small" you will discover success. You'll quickly find out that the big things come along just when they are ready.

Conclusion

So you've reached the end of the book and I sincerely hope it has started you on the road to riding out on your horse. You've looked at a huge variety of obstacles as simple as walking over a pole to trotting under low branches, to challenging yourself to gallop through the waves on a beach. It is impossible to cover every situation and obstacle you could ever meet but the more you and your horse experience, the safer you both will feel. One day you will find yourself welcoming a challenging encounter out on the trail, and soon you'll be seeking them out. You have the skills now to build a success plan, not because you and your horse think it is the only way to survive, but because it's fun.

Look at our wonderful world, go out, ride there and start to enjoy the journey.

Index

Page numbers in *italics* indicate illustrations.

YE03
XHA